MACMILLAN LITERATURE COLLECTION

Science Fiction Stories

edited by Ceri Jones

Macmillan Education
4 Crinan Street
London N1 9XW
A division of Macmillan Publishers Limited
Companies and representatives throughout the world

ISBN 978–0–2307–1691–9

All additional material written by Ceri Jones

First published 2009
Text © Macmillan Publishers Limited 2009
Design and illustration © Macmillan Publishers Limited 2009

The authors and publishers are grateful for permission to reprint the following
copyright material:

Scovil Chichak Galen Literary Agency, Inc. for the story *We Can Remember It
For You Wholesale* by Philip K Dick copyright © 1966. Reprinted by permission of
the author and the author's agents, Scovil Chichak Galen Literary Agency, Inc;

Don Congdon Associates, Inc. for the story *A Sound of Thunder* by Ray Bradbury
copyright © 1952 by the Crowell Collier Publishing Company, renewed 1980 by
Ray Bradbury. Reprinted by permission of Don Congdon Associates, Inc.;

David Higham Associates Limited for the story *Travel By Wire!* by Arthur C
Clarke from *Arthur C Clarke: The Collected Stories* published by Gollancz.
Reprinted by permission of David Higham Associates Limited.

These materials may contain links for third party websites. We have no control
over, and are not responsible for, the contents of such third party websites. Please
use care when accessing them.

Cover by NASA & Punchstock/Brand X Pictures

Printed and bound in Thailand

2016 2015 2014
11   10   9   8   7   6

Contents

Macmillan Literature Collections

Welcome to the *Macmillan Literature Collections* – a series of advanced-level readers containing original, unsimplified short stories written by famous classic and modern writers. We hope that these stories will help to ease your students' transition from graded readers to reading authentic novels.

Each collection in the series includes:

Introduction

- an introduction to the short story
- tips for reading authentic texts in English
- an introduction to the genre
- a carefully-chosen selection of classic and modern short stories.

The stories

Each story is presented in three parts: the introduction and pre-reading support material; the story; and post-reading activities. Each part includes the following sections:

- *About the author* – in-depth information about the author and their work
- *About the story* – information about the story, including background information about setting and cultural references
- *Summary* – a brief summary of the story that does not give away the ending.

Pre-reading exercises

- *Key vocabulary* – a chance to look at some of the more difficult vocabulary related to the main themes and style of the story before reading the story
- *Main themes* – a brief discussion of the main themes, with questions to keep in mind as you read.

The story

You will find numbered footnotes in the stories. These explain cultural and historical references, and key words that you will need to understand the text. Many of these footnotes give definitions of words which are very formal, old-fashioned or rarely used in modern English. You will find more common, useful words and phrases from the stories in the *Glossary* at the end of the book. Words included in the *Glossary* will appear in **bold**.

Post-reading exercises

- *Understanding the story* – comprehension questions that will help you make sure you've understood the story
- *Language study* – a section that presents and practises key linguistic and structural features of authentic literary texts (you will find an index of the areas covered at the end of the book)
- *Literary analysis* – discussion questions that guide you to an in-depth appreciation of the story, its structure, its characters and its style.

In addition, at the end of each book there are:
- suggested *Essay questions*
- a comprehensive *Glossary* highlighting useful vocabulary from each story
- an **index** for the *Language study* section.

How to use these books

You can use these books in whatever way you want. You may want to start from the beginning and work your way through. You may want to pick and choose. The *Contents* page gives a very brief, one-line introduction to each story to help you decide where to start. You may want to learn about the author and the story before you read each one, or you may prefer to read the story first and then find out more about it afterwards. Remember that the stories and exercises can be challenging, so you may want to spend quite a long time studying each one. The most important thing is to enjoy the collection – to enjoy reading, to enjoy the stories and to enjoy the language that has been used to create them.

—

Answer keys

In many cases you can check your answers in the story by using the page references given. However, an Answer key for all the exercises will be available on the student's section of the Macmillan Readers website at www.macmillanenglish.com/readers

Introduction

What is a short story?

A short story is shorter than a novel, but longer than a poem. It is usually between 1,000 and 20,000 words long. It tells a story which can usually be read quite quickly. It often concentrates on one, central event; it has a limited number of characters, and takes place within a short space of time.

History of the short story

Stories and storytelling have existed for as long as people have had language. People love, and need, stories. They help us explain and understand the world. Before people could read or write, storytellers travelled from village to village, telling stories.

The first written stories developed from this storytelling tradition. Two of the best-known examples of early, written stories in Europe appeared in the 14th century. Chaucer's *Canterbury Tales* and Bocaccio's *Decameron* are both based on the same idea – a group of people who are travelling or living together for a short time, agree to tell each other stories.

The first modern short stories appeared at the beginning of the 19th century. Early examples of short-story collections include the *Fairy Tales* (1824–26) of the Brothers Grimm, and Edgar Allan Poe's *Tales of the Grotesque and Arabesque* (1840). In the late 19th century, printed magazines and journals became very popular and more and more short stories were published. By the 20th century most well-known magazines included short stories in every issue and the publishers paid a lot of money for them. In 1952 Ernest Hemingway's short story, *The Old Man and the Sea*, helped sell more than five million copies of the magazine *Life* in just two days.

The short story today

Today, short stories are often published in collections called anthologies. They are usually grouped according to a particular category – by theme, topic, national origin, time, or author. Some newspapers and magazines continue to print individual stories. Many short stories are first published on the Internet, with authors posting them on special-interest websites and in online magazines.

Reading authentic literary texts in English

Reading authentic literary texts can be difficult. They may contain grammatical structures you have not studied, or expressions and sayings you are not familiar with. Unlike graded readers, they have not been written for language students. The words have been chosen to create a particular effect, not because they are easy or difficult. But you do not need to understand every word to understand and enjoy the story.

When you are reading in your own language you will often read so quickly that you skip over words, and read for the general effect, rather than the details. Try to do the same when you are reading in English. Remember that looking up every word you don't know slows you down and stops you enjoying the story.

When you're reading authentic short stories, remember:
– It should be a pleasure!
– You should read at your own pace.
– Let the story carry you along – don't worry about looking up every word you don't understand.
– Don't worry about looking up difficult words unless they stop you from understanding the story.
– Try not to use the *Glossary* or a dictionary when you're reading.

You might want to make a note of words to look up later, especially key words that you see several times (see *Using a dictionary* on page 9 for more tips on looking up and recording new words). But remember, you can always go back again when you have finished the story. That is the beauty of reading short stories – they are short! You can finish one quite quickly, especially if you do not worry about understanding every single word; then you can start again at the beginning and take your time to re-read difficult passages and look up key words.

Preparing yourself for a story

It is always a good idea to prepare yourself, mentally, before starting a story.
– Look at the title. What does it tell you about the story? What do you expect the story to be about?
– If there is a summary, read it. This will help you follow the story.

- Quickly read the first few paragraphs and answer these questions:
  Where is it set?
  When is it set?
  Who is the main character?
- As you read, concentrate on following the gist (the general idea) of the story. You can go back and look at the details later. You can use the questions at the end of the story (see *Understanding the story*) to help you understand what is happening.

Tips for dealing with difficult passages

Some stories include particularly difficult passages. They are usually descriptive and give background information, or set the scene. They are generally difficult to follow because they are full of detail. Try to read these passages quickly, understanding what you can, and then continue with the story. Make a note of the passage and come back to it later, when you have finished the whole story.

If, at any time, you are finding it difficult to follow the story, go back to this difficult passage. It may hold the answers to your questions.

Read through the passage again carefully and underline all the unknown words. Try to understand as much as you can from the immediate context and what you now know about the story. Then, look up any remaining words in the *Glossary* at the back of the book, or in your dictionary.

Tips for dealing with difficult words

- Decide if the word (or phrase) is important to the overall message. Read the whole paragraph. Do you understand the general meaning? Yes? Then the word isn't important. Don't worry about it. *Keep reading!*
- If you decide the word is important, see if you can work out its meaning from the context. Is it a verb, a noun or an adjective? Is it positive or negative? How would you translate it into in your own language? Underline the word or make a note of it and the page number, but *keep reading*. If it really is important, you'll see it again.
- If you keep seeing the same word in the story, and you still can't understand it, look in your monolingual dictionary!

Using a dictionary

Looking up words

Before you look up the word, look at it again in its context. Decide what part of speech it is. Try to guess its meaning from the context. Now look it up in your dictionary. There may be more than one definition given. Decide which one is the most appropriate. If the word is something very specific, eg the name of a flower or tree, you can use a bilingual dictionary to give you the exact translation.

Let's look at how this works in practice. Look at this short extract and follow the instructions below.

> ...there is a little valley or rather **lap** of land among high hills, which is one of the quietest places in the whole world. A small **brook** glides through it, with just murmur enough to **lull** one to repose*
>
> *literary: sleep or rest*
> The Legend of Sleepy Hollow by Washington Irvine

1 Look at the words in bold and decide what part of speech they are – noun, verb, adjective, etc.
2 Try to guess what they might mean.
3 Look at the extracts below from the *Macmillan English Dictionary for Advanced Learners*. Choose the most appropriate definition.

Words with more than one entry Sometimes the same word belongs to more than one word class: for example, *brook* can be both a noun and a verb. Each word class is shown as a separate entry. The small number at the end of the head-word tells you that a word has more than one entry.	**brook¹** noun
	 a small river
	 brook² verb
	    not brook – to definitely not allow or accept something.
	 lap¹ noun
	    1 the top half of your legs above your knees when you sit down.
	    2 one complete turn around a course in a race
	    PHRASE in the lap of luxury in very comfortable and expensive conditions

Idioms and fixed expressions Some words are often used in idioms and fixed expressions. These are shown at the end of the entry, following the small box that says PHRASE.	**lap²** verb
	    1 if an animal laps water, it drinks it gently with its tongue
	 lull¹ noun
	    a quiet period during a very active or violent situation

Words with more than one meaning Many words have more than one meaning, and each different meaning is shown by a number.	**lull²** verb
	    1 to make someone feel relaxed and confident so that they are not prepared for something unpleasant to happen to lull someone into a false sense of security
	    2 to make someone relaxed enough to go to sleep

Dictionary extracts adapted from the Macmillan English Dictionary © Macmillan Publishers Limited 2002

Keeping a record

When you have looked in your dictionary, decide if the word is interesting or useful to you. If it is, make a note of it, and write down its definition. Make a note of the sentence where you found it in the story, then write one or two more examples of your own. Only do this for those words you think you will need to use in the future.

Here is an example of how you might record the word *lull*.

'with just murmur enough to lull one to repose'
Lull – to make you feel relaxed enough to go to sleep
e.g. The quiet sound of the waves lulled me to sleep
The mother sang to her baby to lull it to sleep

Literary analysis

The *Literary analysis* section is written to encourage you to consider the stories in more depth. This will help you to appreciate them better and develop your analytical skills. This section is particularly useful for those students who are studying, or intending to study, literature in the medium of English. Each section includes literary terms with which you may or may not be familiar.

Macmillan Readers student's site

For more help with understanding these literary terms, and to find Answer keys to all the exercises and activities, visit the student's section of the Macmillan Readers' website at www.macmillanenglish. com/readers. There you will also find a wealth of resources to help your language learning in English; from listening exercises to articles on acedemic and creative writing.

The genre of Science Fiction

What is science fiction?

Science fiction is a genre that explores the influence of science and technology on people and society. It does not describe science as we know and use it in reality, but explores imaginary, future scientific and technological developments.

Hard science fiction

Science-fiction stories are often set in the future, and predict how technological changes will change the world we live in. Science fiction of this type has often successfully predicted real scientific developments and new technologies. For example, H G Wells predicted that man would one day walk on the moon in 1901, almost 70 years before it actually happened, and Arthur C Clarke described an idea very similar to the Internet, a 'global library', in a book published in 1962. Science-fiction stories that base themselves on detailed knowledge of current scientific developments are often called 'hard' science fiction.

Soft science fiction

Some other science-fiction stories are set in an alternative parallel time and explore a 'what if' situation. For example, what if Martians landed on Earth, what would happen, how would we communicate with them? Or what if there was a device that allowed us to read other people's minds, how would this affect our lives? This kind of science fiction, which is interested in exploring how society works and in commenting on human behaviour, is often called 'soft' science fiction.

Science fiction, sci-fi or SF?

The term *science fiction* was first abbreviated to *sci-fi* in the 1950s in the USA. However, the term soon came to be used to talk about low-quality science-fiction stories and low-budget science-fiction films, and to distinguish between serious, high-quality science-fiction and poor quality, cheap sci-fi. Nowadays, serious science-fiction authors refer to the genre, and themselves, with the initials SF.

The origins of science fiction

Ideas about the possibility of flying machines, alien races and advanced civilisations have existed throughout the history of literature. In early Arabic literature there are examples of space travel and other advanced technologies. In early Hindu writings there are descriptions of flying machines and submarines. Literary critics have argued that both Dante and Shakespeare used elements of science fiction in their work.

Early science fiction

In the 16th and 17th centuries, scientists such as Galileo and Newton revolutionised the world of science. Writers throughout Europe took up their ideas and wrote about the possibilities of space travel, alternative worlds and alien cultures. Cyrano de Bergerac wrote about travelling to the moon in 1656. Jonathan Swift wrote about alien cultures in *Gulliver's Travels* in 1726.

Probably the best-known early science-fiction work in English is Mary Shelley's *Frankenstein*, published in 1818. Although it is usually classified as a horror story, it also contains key elements of science-fiction. The creation of the monster is based on scientific principles, its creator is a scientist, and the story explores the terrible consequences of pushing science beyond its normal limits. These are all themes which are seen again and again in science-fiction literature.

The fathers of modern science fiction

Jules Verne and H G Wells were probably the two most influential early science-fiction writers. Verne's most famous stories, *Journey to the Centre of the Earth* (1864), *From Earth to the Moon* (1865) and *Twenty Thousand Leagues Under the Sea* (1870) were very successful and some believe that he was the first successful, full-time science-fiction novelist. He wrote in French and he is the third most-translated author of all time, according to the UNESCO translations index.

H G Wells's early novels, *The Time Machine*, *The Invisible Man* and *The First Men on the Moon* introduced a number of themes that are now classics of science fiction. His novel *The War of the Worlds*, which describes a Martian invasion of Earth, has also become a classic, as has *The Island of Dr Thoreau*, which explores the themes of vivisection (animal experiments) and genetic engineering (experimenting with human, animal and plant genes). He and Verne are both often called the 'fathers of science fiction'.

Science fiction in the 20th century

Cheap science-fiction magazines helped the science-fiction genre to develop and grow in the early 20th century.

One magazine in particular in the USA had a very strong influence on the genre: *Astounding Science Fiction*, founded in 1930. Its editor, John W Campbell, brought together a group of very influential writers, including Isaac Asimov, Arthur C Clarke and Robert Heinlein. This was the beginning of the Golden Age of science fiction in the USA. Campbell's insistence on scientific detail meant science fiction started to be taken more seriously as a genre.

Political changes and scientific developments throughout the 20th century led to a number of developments in science fiction. Writers in the 1950s and 60s wrote about secret groups, police states and alternative realities. In the 1970s, new themes included environmental issues and the question of mind control. In the 1980s, authors started to write about computers, and in the 1990s, nanotechnology (building small machines using computer technology), artificial intelligence (computers which can think like human beings) and the influence of the Internet all became important new themes to explore.

Science fiction today

Science fiction continues to develop and explore new themes and discoveries in the 21st century. The Internet has become important for the genre, with hundreds of thousands of websites dedicated to science fiction. Many new authors publish their stories online.

We Can Remember It For You Wholesale
by Philip K Dick

About the author

Philip Kindred Dick was a US science-fiction novelist and short story writer. He is best known for the stories that inspired famous science fiction films such as *Blade Runner* (1982), *Total Recall* (1990) and *Minority Report* (2002). In 2007, he became the first science-fiction writer to be included in The Library of America[1] series.

Philip K Dick was born in Chicago in December 1928, one of twins, but his twin sister, Jane, died after only six weeks. The death of his sister had a deep effect on him, and can be seen in the repeated theme of the 'phantom twin' in many of his books.

When Philip was still at elementary school the family moved to California, which became his lifelong home. After leaving school he attended Berkeley University for a brief time, but gave up without completing any coursework. During the same period he suffered mental health problems and was diagnosed with schizophrenia. The theme of double or multiple identities runs through his work.

Philip read his first science-fiction story when he was twelve and immediately fell in love with the genre. He was fascinated by the world of science and the exploration of futuristic worlds. When he first left school he worked in a record shop, but after four years, in 1952, he sold his first science-fiction story and left his job to become a full-time writer.

He went on to write more than 120 stories, most of them for science fiction magazines. In the first two years of his career, from 1952–53, he wrote 67 stories, five of which have been made into films. His first novel, *Solar Lottery*, was published in 1955. He went on to write more than 40 novels. Like many science-fiction writers, he wrote at an incredible rate and between 1959 and 1964, he wrote and published 17 science-fiction novels.

In 1963, Dick won the Hugo Award[2] for best novel with *The Man in*

---

1 A non- profit organisation which has as its mission to preserve the USA's cultural heritage by publishing the USA's best and most significant works of literature.
2 The Hugo Awards are awarded each year for the best science fiction/fantasy fiction of the previous year.

the High Castle and in 1975 *Flow My Tears, The Policeman Said* won the John W Campbell Memorial Award[3] for best novel.

The Philip K Dick Award is now an annual science-fiction award which is presented to the best original science-fiction paperback published each year in the USA.

About the story

We Can Remember It For You Wholesale was first published in *The Magazine of Fantasy & Science Fiction* in April 1966. The story is included in the short-story collection of the same name. It was the inspiration for the 1990 action movie *Total Recall*, starring Arnold Schwarzenegger.

The story is set in Chicago in the future. No exact date is given. The government on Earth (*Terra*, as it is called in the story) has sent people to live on Mars. Taxis are driven by robots. People can go on holiday under the sea thanks to special suits that help them breathe underwater. Companies sell false memories of adventures and holidays. The secret police use special *telepathic transmitters* to read the thoughts of their agents.

Background information

Mars

The few details the story contains about Mars and possible life on Mars are true to knowledge of the planet at the time. It was believed that there might be water somewhere on the surface and that its basic characteristics meant that life was possible there.

The atmosphere on Mars was known to be much thinner than on Earth and observations of the planet showed enormous craters, valleys and mountains on its surface. Mars was known to have two moons, which are referred to in the story, as is the origin of the planet's name: the Roman God of War.

(For more information about Mars, see the notes in the *Background information* section for *The Martian Odyssey*.)

---

3 One of the three major, annual awards for science fiction (the others are the Hugo and the Nebula Awards).

Truth drugs

The drug that Rekal use before they implant their clients' false memories is based on the idea of a truth drug, a drug which forces people to tell the truth. Most known truth drugs are based on sedatives. The use of these drugs is classified as a form of torture under international law. It is believed that many secret-police organisations have used, and continue to use, these kinds of drugs when trying to obtain information.

Summary

It may help you to know something about what happens in the story before you read it. Don't worry, this summary does *not* tell you how the story ends!

Douglas Quail is an office worker. He is bored with his day-to-day working life and dreams of going to Mars. But on his office worker's salary he cannot afford to go, since it is far too expensive. His wife tries to persuade him to take a trip to an undersea resort, but he is obsessed by the idea of going to Mars, so much so that he even dreams about it at night.

Finally, one day he decides to visit a company called Rekal, a company which sells memories. He wants to buy the memory of a trip to Mars, but not as a simple tourist. He wants to buy a memory of a trip to Mars as a government secret agent. The company are able to do this, and although Quail has some doubts, he decides to buy the trip.

But when the technicians try to implant the memory they discover a problem. Under the influence of the drugs used by the Rekal technicians Quail remembers a real trip to Mars. The government had tried to erase the memory, but the drugs used by Rekal have brought it back. The technicians decide that the safest thing to do is to bring Quail out of sedation without implanting the false memory.

On the way home in a taxi, Quail at first thinks that he's just come back from Mars, but then he finds a letter for Rekal in his pocket and he remembers the failed implant. He is angry and goes back to complain. At Rekal the boss gives him back his money and advises him not to talk about his memories of Mars.

When he gets home he discovers a box of worms that he had

brought back from Mars with him. He is confused, he doesn't know if his memories are real or false. He asks his wife, hoping that she will be able to help him, but she walks out on him.

A member of the Interplan police agency enters the flat. He has a gun in his hand. He explains that Quail had in fact been to Mars on a secret mission, a mission so secret that if he remembers it they will be forced to kill him. Unfortunately, the conversation with the police agents helps Quail remember more and more details about his trip to Mars. The agents try to kill Quail in his flat, but he manages to escape.

However, Quail realises that he cannot hide from the police for long so he reaches an agreement with the Interplan agents that will save his life. He will have a new false memory implanted, one which is even more exciting than the trip to Mars. A psychiatrist helps identify Quail's most intimate fantasy, and Quail returns to Rekal to have his fantasy implanted as a false memory. But back at Rekal, things do not go as planned.

Pre-reading exercises

Key vocabulary

This section will help you familiarise yourself with some of the more specific vocabulary used in the story. You may want to use it to help you before you start reading, or as a revision exercise after you have finished the story.

Words that were invented for the purpose of the story

1 **Look at the words in the box. They are all words that have been invented for the story. What do you think they might be? Match them to the definitions below. Use the notes to help you.**

conapt   foot runnel   gill[a] outfit   homeopapes   maw-worms[c]
narkidrine   poscreds   sneaky-pete[b] guns   traffic runnel

a) an apartment in a condominium[d]
b) a tunnel-like bridge for cars
c) a tunnel-like bridge for pedestrians
d) a suit which allows you to breathe under water
e) some form of money

f) a weapon that is hidden from sight

g) a drug which is used both to sedate and to force people to tell the truth

h) a simple life form found on Mars

i) a form of futuristic newspaper service

Notes

a one of the organs behind the head of a fish that allow it to breathe

b sneaky-pete notes are used by students who want to cheat in an exam

c creatures with a long, soft body and no bones or legs

d a building that contains several flats, each owned by the people who live there

---

Notice how the writer combines words that are familiar to create the new words, eg run + tunnel = runnel, or home + video = homeo. What other combinations can you see?

2 Use the words in the box above to complete these extracts from the story.

1 He made his way barefoot from the bedroom of their .... to the kitchen.

2 'Yes,' he said and gazed out the kitchen window at the hovercars and .... , and all the little energetic people hurrying to work.

3 Rent an artificial .... for both of us, take a week off from work, and we can descend and live down there at one of those year-round aquatic resorts.

4 Douglas Quail slowly walked across three densely-populated .... and to the modern, attractively inviting doorway.

5 Quail is already under sedation; he reacted well to the .... ; he's completely unconscious and receptive.

6 Reaching into his coat pocket ... he discovered ... that it contained five hundred and seventy .... , in 'cred bills of low denomination.

7 Opening the box he saw, to his disbelief, six dead .... and several varieties of the unicellular life on which the Martian worms fed.

8 The Interplan police used them; that had come out even in the news in the ....

9 Some armed with .... , the way you are.

Idiomatic expressions

3 Dick uses a number of informal, idiomatic expressions in his writing. Look at the expressions below and their definitions. Use them to complete the extracts below.

at stake likely to be lost or damaged if something fails
bread and butter something that provides your main income
bring someone (back down) to earth to make someone suddenly remember the real situation after they have been so excited or happy that they forgot
fool around with something to handle something in a stupid or careless way
run into trouble to start to have problems
song-and-dance an elaborate effort to explain or justify something

1 Everything conspired to remind him of what he was. A miserable little salaried employee, he said to himself with bitterness. Kirsten reminded him of this at least once a day and he did not blame her; it was a wife's job to .... her husband ....

2 'You may go ahead, Lowe; I don't think you'll .... any ....'

3 In one month, he calculated wryly, we must do twenty of these ... interplanetary travel has become our ....

4 'The less we mess with this man,' McClane said, 'the better I like it. This is nothing for us to .... ; we've been foolish enough to – or unlucky enough to – uncover a genuine Interplan spy.'

5 All that .... you went into – it hasn't materialized into a damn thing.

6 A secret and dangerous trip to Mars in which his life was .... – everything he had wanted as a false memory.

Main themes

Before you read the story, you may want to think about some of its main themes. The questions will help you think about the story as you are reading it for the first time. There is more discussion of the main themes in in the *Literary analysis* section after the story.

What is real?

One of the main themes of Philip K Dick's writings is that of the nature of reality. How do we know what is real and what is false? In *We Can Remember It For You Wholesale*, the problem is complex. Slowly, as the story develops, Douglas Quail is forced to question everything, himself, his wife, his memories.

4 As you read the story, think about these questions:

a) Which of his memories are true?
b) How do we know?
c) How does he know?

Multiple identities

The theme of multiple identities is another theme that runs through all of Dick's works. In *We Can Remember It For You Wholesale*, both Douglas Quail and his wife seem to have multiple identities.

5 As you read the story, think about these questions:

a) What are Douglas Quail's various different identities?
b) Which is the real Douglas Quail?
c) Is there a real Douglas Quail?
d) What about his wife? What are her different identities?

Memories

The story invites us to explore the nature of memories. What are they? Can they be trusted? How are they created?

6 As you read the story, think about these questions:

a) What's the difference between a real memory and the memories sold by Rekal?
b) How can we know if our memories are real, or if they have been affected by the passage of time, or influenced by other people's perceptions and accounts of events?

We Can Remember It For You Wholesale

by Philip K Dick

1

He awoke – and wanted Mars. The valleys, he thought. What would it be like to **trudge** among them? Great and greater yet: the dream grew as he became fully conscious, the dream and the **yearning**. He could almost feel the enveloping presence of the other world, which only Government agents and high officials had seen. A clerk like himself? Not likely.

'Are you getting up or not?' his wife Kirsten asked **drowsily**, with her usual hint of fierce **crossness**. 'If you are, push the hot coffee button on the darn[4] stove.'

'Okay,' Douglas Quail said, and made his way barefoot from the bedroom of their conapt to the kitchen. There, having dutifully pressed the hot coffee button, he seated himself at the kitchen table, brought out a yellow, small tin of fine Dean Swift snuff[5]. He inhaled briskly, and the Beau Nash mixture stung his nose, burned the roof his mouth. But still he inhaled; it woke him up and allowed his dreams, his nocturnal desires and random wishes, to condense into a semblance of rationality.

I will go, he said to himself. *Before I die I'll see Mars.*

It was, of course, impossible, and he knew this even as he dreamed. But the daylight, the **mundane** noise of his wife now brushing her hair before the bedroom mirror – everything conspired to remind him of what he was. *A miserable little salaried employee*, he said to himself with bitterness. Kirsten reminded him of this at least once a day and he did not blame her; it was a wife's job to bring her husband down to Earth. *Down to Earth*, he thought, and

4 *informal, mainly* US: used when you are annoyed about something
5 tobacco in the form of a powder that you breathe in through your nose

laughed. The figure of speech in this was literally apt.

'What are you **sniggering** about?' his wife asked as she swept into the kitchen, her long busy-pink robe wagging after her. 'A dream, I bet. You're always full of them.'

'Yes,' he said, and gazed out the kitchen window at the hovercars and traffic runnels, and all the little energetic people hurrying to work. In a little while he would be among them. As always.

'I'll bet it had to do with some women,' Kirsten said witheringly.

'No,' he said. 'A god. The god of war. He has wonderful craters with every kind of plant-life growing deep down in them.'

'Listen.' Kirsten **crouched down** beside him and spoke earnestly, the harsh quality momentarily gone from her voice. 'The bottom of the ocean – *our* ocean is much more, an infinity of times more beautiful. You know that; everyone knows that. Rent an artificial gill-outfit for both of us, take a week off from work, and we can descend and live down there at one of those year-round aquatic resorts. And in addition – ' She broke off. 'You're not listening. You should be. Here is something a lot better than that compulsion, that obsession you have about Mars, and you don't even listen!' Her voice rose piercingly. 'God in heaven, you're **doomed**, Doug! What's going to become of you?'

'I'm going to work,' he said, rising to his feet, his breakfast forgotten. 'That's what's going to become of me.'

She eyed him. 'You're getting worse. More fanatical every day. Where's it going to lead?'

'To Mars,' he said, and opened the door to the closet[6] to get down a fresh shirt to wear to work.

2

Having descended from the taxi Douglas Quail slowly walked across three densely-populated foot runnels and to the modern, attractively inviting doorway. There he halted, **impeding** midmorning traffic, and with caution read the shifting-colour

6 US: wardrobe (a cupboard for keeping clothes in)

neon sign. He had, in the past, **scrutinized** this sign before …
but never had he come so close. This was very different; what he
did now was something else. Something which sooner or later
had to happen.

Was this the answer? After all, an illusion, no matter how
convincing, remained nothing more than an illusion. At least
objectively. But subjectively – quite the opposite entirely.

And anyhow he had an appointment. Within the next five
minutes.

Taking a deep breath of mildly smog-infested Chicago air,
he walked through the dazzling **polychromatic shimmer** of the
doorway and up to the receptionist's counter.

The nicely-articulated blonde at the counter, bare-bosomed
and tidy, said pleasantly, 'Good morning, Mr Quail.'

'Yes,' he said. 'I'm here to see about a Rekal course. As I guess
you know.'

'Not "rekal" but *recall*,' the receptionist corrected him. She
picked up the receiver of the vidphone by her smooth elbow and
said into it, 'Mr Douglas Quail is here, Mr McClane. May he
come inside, now? Or is it too soon?'

'Giz wetwa wum-wum wamp,' the phone **mumbled**.

'Yes, Mr Quail,' she said. 'You may go in; Mr McClane is
expecting you.' As he started off uncertainly she called after
him, 'Room D, Mr Quail. To your right.'

After a frustrating but brief moment of being lost he found the
proper room. The door hung open and inside, at a big genuine
walnut desk, sat a genial-looking man, middle-aged, wearing the
latest Martian frog-pelt gray[7] suit; his **attire** alone would have
told Quail that he had come to the right person.

'Sit down, Douglas,' McClane said, waving his plump hand
toward a chair which faced the desk. 'So you want to have gone
to Mars. Very good.'

Quail seated himself, feeling tense. 'I'm not so sure this is
worth the fee,' he said. 'It costs a lot and as far as I can see I
really get nothing.' *Costs almost as much as going*, he thought.

'You get tangible proof of your trip,' McClane disagreed

7 *US spelling*: British spelling is *grey*

emphatically. 'All the proof you'll need. Here; I'll show you,' He dug within a drawer of his impressive desk. 'Ticket stub.' Reaching into a manila[8] folder, he produced a small square of **embossed** cardboard. 'It proves you went – and returned. Postcards.' He laid out four **franked** picture 3-D full-colour postcards in a neatly-arranged row on the desk for Quail to see. 'Film. Shots you took of local sights on Mars with a rented moving camera.' To Quail he displayed those, too. 'Plus the name of the people you met, two hundred poscreds worth of souvenirs, which will arrive – from Mars – within the following month. And passport, certificates listing the shots[9] you received. And more.' He glanced up keenly at Quail. 'You'll know you went, all right,' he said. 'You won't remember us, won't remember me or ever having been here. It'll be a real trip in your mind; we guarantee that. A full two weeks of recall; every last piddling[10] detail. Remember this: if at any time you doubt that you really took an extensive trip to Mars you can return here and get a full refund. You see?'

'But I didn't go,' Quail said. 'I won't have gone, no matter what proofs you provide me with.' He took a deep, unsteady breath. 'And I never was a secret agent with Interplan.' It seemed impossible to him that Rekal Incorporated's extra-factual memory implant would do its job – despite what he had heard people say.

'Mr Quail,' McClane said patiently. 'As you explained in your letter to us, you have no chance, no possibility in the slightest, of ever actually getting to Mars; you can't afford it, and what is much more important, you could never qualify as an undercover agent for Interplan or anybody else. This is the only way you can achieve your, ahem, life-long dream; am I not correct, sir? You can't be this; you can't actually do this' He chuckled. 'But you can *have been* and *have done*. We see to that. And our fee is reasonable; no hidden charges.' He smiled encouragingly.

'Is an extra-factual memory that convincing?' Quail asked.

8 made of strong, light brown paper
9 vaccinations
10 *informal:* small or unimportant

'More than the real thing, sir. Had you really gone to Mars as an Interplan agent, you would by now have forgotten a great deal; our analysis of true-mem systems – authentic recollections of major events in a person's life – shows that a variety of details are very quickly lost to the person. Forever. Part of the package we offer you is such deep implantation of recall that nothing is forgotten. The packet which is fed to you while you're comatose is the creation of trained experts, men who have spent years on Mars; in every case we verify details down to the last iota. And you've picked a rather easy extra-factual system; had you picked Pluto or wanted to be Emperor of the Inner Planet Alliance we'd have much more difficulty ... and the charges would be considerably greater.'

Reaching into his coat for his wallet, Quail said, 'Okay. It's been my life-long ambition and so I see I'll never really do it. So I guess I'll have to settle for this.'

'Don't think of it that way,' McClane said severely. 'You're not accepting second-best. The actual memory, with all its vagueness, omissions and **ellipses**, not to say distortions – that's second-best.' He accepted the money and pressed a button on his desk. 'All right. Mr Quail,' he said, as the door of his office opened and two **burly** men swiftly entered. 'You're on your way to Mars as a secret agent.' He rose, came over to shake Quail's nervous, moist hand. 'Or rather, you have been on your way. This afternoon at four-thirty you will, um, arrive back here on Terra; a cab will leave you off at your conapt and as I say you will never remember seeing me or coming here; you won't, in fact, even remember having heard of our existence.'

His mouth dry with nervousness, Quail followed the two technicians from the office; what happened next depended on them.

Will I actually believe I've been to Mars? He wondered. *That I managed to fulfil my lifetime ambition?* He had a strange, **lingering** intuition that something would go wrong. But just what – he did not know.

He would have to wait and find out.

The intercom on McClane's desk, which connected him with the work area of the firm, buzzed and a voice said, 'Mr Quail is under sedation now, sir. Do you want to supervise this one, or shall we go ahead?'

'It's routine,' McClane observed. 'You may go ahead, Lowe; I don't think you'll run into any trouble.' Programming an artificial memory of a trip to another planet – with or without the added fillip[11] of being a secret agent – showed up on the firm's work-schedule with monotonous regularity. *In one month*, he calculated wryly, *we must do twenty of these …ersatz[12] interplanetary travel has become our bread and butter.*

'Whatever you say, Mr McClane,' Lowe's voice came, and thereupon the intercom shut off.

Going to the vault section in the chamber behind his office, McClane searched about for a Three packet – trip to Mars – and a Sixty-two packet: secret Interplan spy. Finding the two packets, he returned with them to his desk, seated himself comfortably, poured out the contents – merchandise which would be planted in Quail's conapt while the lab technicians busied themselves installing the false memory.

A one-poscred sneaky-pete side arm, McClane reflected; *that's the largest item. Sets us back financially the most.* Then a pellet-sized transmitter, which could be swallowed if the agent were caught. Code book that astonishingly resembled the real thing … the firm's models were highly accurate: based, whenever possible, on actual US military issue. Odd bits which made no intrinsic sense but which would be woven into the warp and woof[13] of Quail's imaginary trip, would coincide with his memory: half an ancient silver fifty cent piece, several quotations from John Donne[14]'s sermons written incorrectly, each on a separate piece of transparent tissue-thin paper, several match folders from bars on Mars, a stainless steel spoon engraved PROPERTY OF

11 something that improves a situation
12 used instead of something better or more expensive
13 the essential, basic structure of something
14 a 17th-century English metaphysical poet

DOME-MARS NATIONAL KIBBUZIM, a wire tapping coil[15] which –

The intercom buzzed. 'Mr McClane, I'm sorry to bother you but something rather **ominous** has come up. Maybe it would be better if you were in here after all. Quail is already under sedation; he reacted well to the narkidrine; he's completely unconscious and receptive. But – '

'I'll be in.' Sensing trouble, McClane left his office; a moment later he emerged in the work area.

On a hygienic bed lay Douglas Quail, breathing slowly and regularly, his eyes virtually shut; he seemed dimly – but only dimly – aware of the two technicians and now McClane himself.

'There's no space to insert false memory-patterns?' McClane felt irritation. 'Merely drop out two work weeks; he's employed as a clerk at the West Coast Emigration Bureau, which is a government agency, so he undoubtedly has or had two weeks' vacation[16] within the last year. That ought to do it.' Petty details annoyed him. And always would.

'Our problem,' Lowe said sharply, 'is something quite different.' He bent over the bed, said to Quail, 'Tell Mr McClane what you told us.' To McClane he said, 'Listen closely.'

The gray-green eyes of the man lying supine in the bed focussed on McClane's face. The eyes, he observed uneasily, had become hard; they had a polished, inorganic quality, like semi-precious tumbled stones. He was not sure that he liked what he saw; the brilliance was too cold. 'What do you want now?' Quail said harshly. 'You've broken my cover. Get out of here before I take you all apart.' He studied McClane. 'Especially you,' he continued. 'You're in charge of this counter-operation.'

Lowe said, 'How long were you on Mars?'

'One month,' Quail said gratingly.

'And your purpose there?' Lowe demanded.

The meager[17] lips twisted; Quail eyed him and did not speak.

15 used for recording conversations secretly
16 US: British word is *holiday*
17 US: British spelling is *meagre*

At last, **drawling** the words out so that they dripped with hostility, he said, 'Agent for Interplan. As I already told you. Don't you record everything that's said? Play your vid-aud tape back for your boss and leave me alone.' He shut his eyes, then; the hard brilliance ceased. McClane felt, instantly, a rushing splurge of relief.

Lowe said quietly, 'This is a tough man, Mr McClane.'

'He won't be,' McClane said, 'after we arrange for him to lose his memory-chain again. He'll be as meek as before.' To Quail he said, 'So *this* is why you wanted to go to Mars so terribly bad.'

Without opening his eyes Quail said, 'I never wanted to go to Mars. I was assigned it – they handed it to me and there I was: stuck. Oh yeah, I admit I was curious about it; who wouldn't be?' Again he opened his eyes and surveyed the three of them, McClane in particular. 'Quite a truth drug you've got here; it brought up things I had absolutely no memory of.' He **pondered**. 'I wonder about Kirsten,' he said, half to himself. 'Could she be in on it? An Interplan contact keeping an eye on me … to be certain I didn't regain my memory? No wonder she's been so derisive about my wanting to go there.' Faintly, he smiled; the smile – one of understanding – disappeared almost at once.

McClane said, 'Please believe me, Mr Quail; we stumbled onto this entirely by accident. In the work we do – '

'I believe you,' Quail said. He seemed tired, no; the drug was continuing to pull him under, deeper and deeper. 'Where did I say I'd been?' he murmured. 'Mars? Hard to remember – I know I'd like to see it; so would everybody else. But me –' His voice trailed off. 'Just a clerk, a nothing clerk.'

Straightening up, Lowe said to his superior. 'He wants a false memory implanted that corresponds to a trip he actually took. And a false reason which is the real reason. He's telling the truth; he's a long way down in the narkidrine. The trip is very vivid in his mind – at least under sedation. But apparently he doesn't recall it otherwise. Someone, probably at a government military-sciences lab, erased his conscious memories; all he knew was that going to Mars meant something special to him, and so did being a secret agent. They wouldn't erase that; it's not a memory but a desire, undoubtedly the same one that motivated him to volunteer for the assignment in the first place.'

The other technician, Keeler, said to McClane, 'What do we do? Graft a false memory-pattern over the real memory? There's no telling what the results would be; he might remember some of the genuine trip, and the confusion might bring on a psychotic interlude[18]. He'd have to hold two opposite premises in his mind simultaneously: that he went to Mars and that he didn't. That he's a genuine agent for Interplan and he's not, that it's **spurious**. I think we ought to revive him without any false memory implantation and send him out of here; this is hot[19].'

'Agreed,' McClane said. A thought came to him. 'Can you predict what he'll remember when he comes out of sedation?'

'Impossible to tell,' Lowe said. 'He probably will have some dim, diffuse memory of his actual trip, now. And he'd probably be in grave doubt as to its validity; he'd probably decide our programming slipped a gear-tooth[20]. And he'd remember coming here; that wouldn't be erased – unless you want it erased.'

'The less we mess with this man,' McClane said, 'the better I like it. This is nothing for us to fool around with; we've been foolish enough to – or unlucky enough to – uncover a genuine Interplan spy who has a cover so perfect that up to now even he didn't know what he was – or rather is.' The sooner they washed their hands of the man calling himself Douglas Quail the better.

'Are you going to plant packets Three and Sixty-two in his conapt?' Lowe said.

'No,' McClane said. 'And we're going to return half his fee.'

'"Half"! Why half?'

McClane said **lamely**, 'It seems to be a good compromise.'

4

As the cab carried him back to his conapt at the residential end of Chicago, Douglas Quail said to himself, *It's sure good to be back on Terra.*

18 uncontrolled violent behaviour
19 *informal:* difficult or dangerous
20 part of a mechanism that helps it function smoothly

Already the month-long period on Mars had begun to waver in his memory; he had only an image of profound gaping craters, and ever-present ancient erosion of hills, of vitality, of motion itself. A world of dust where little happened, where a good part of the day was spent checking and rechecking one's portable oxygen source. And then the life forms, the unassuming and modest gray-brown cacti and maw-worms.

As a matter of fact he had brought back several **moribund** examples of Martian fauna; he had smuggled them through customs. After all, they posed no menace; they couldn't survive in Earth's heavy atmosphere.

Reaching into his coat pocket, he rummaged for the container of Martian maw-worms –

And found an envelope instead.

Lifting it out, he discovered, to his perplexity, that it contained five hundred and seventy poscreds, in 'cred bills of low denomination.

Where'd I get this? he asked himself. *Didn't I spend every 'cred I had on my trip?*

With the money came a slip of paper marked: *One-half fee ret'd. By McClane.* And then the date. Today's date.

'Recall,' he said aloud.

'Recall what, sir or madam?' the robot driver of the cab inquired respectfully.

'Do you have a phone book?' Quail demanded.

'Certainly, sir or madam.' A slot opened; from it slid a microtape phone book of Cook County.

'It's spelled oddly,' Quail said as he leafed through the pages of the yellow section. He felt fear, then; abiding fear. 'Here it is,' he said. 'Take me there, to Rekal, Incorporated. I've changed my mind; I don't want to go home.'

'Yes, sir or madam, as the case may be,' the driver said. A moment later the cab was zipping back in the opposite direction.

'May I make use of your phone?' he asked.

'Be my guest,' the robot driver said. And presented a shiny new emperor 3-D color phone to him.

He **dialled** his own conapt. And after a pause found himself confronted by a miniature but chillingly realistic image of Kirsten on the small screen. 'I've been to Mars,' he said to her.

'You're drunk' Her lips **writhed scornfully**. 'Or worse.'

' 'S God's truth.'

'When?' she demanded.

'I don't know.' He felt confused. 'A simulated trip, I think. By means of one of those artificial or extra-factual or whatever it is memory places. It didn't take.'

Kirsten said witheringly, 'You *are* drunk.' And broke the connection at her end. He hung up, then, feeling his face **flush**. *Always the same tone*, he said hotly to himself. *Always the retort, as if she knows everything and I know nothing. What a marriage. Keerist[21]*, he thought dismally.

A moment later the cab stopped at the curb before a modern, very attractive little pink building, over which a shifting polychromatic neon sign read: REKAL, INCORPORATED.

The receptionist, chic and bare from the waist up, started in surprise, then gained masterful control of herself. 'Oh, hello, Mr Quail,' she said nervously. 'H-how are you? Did you forget something?'

'The rest of my fee back,' he said.

More composed now, the receptionist said, 'Fee? I think you are mistaken, Mr Quail. You were here discussing the feasibility of an extra-factual trip for you, but – ' She shrugged her smooth pale shoulders. 'As I understand it, no trip was taken.'

Quail said, 'I remember everything, miss. My letter to Rekal, Incorporated, which started this whole business off. I remember my arrival here, my visit with Mr McClane. Then the two lab technicians taking me in tow and administering a drug to put me out.' No wonder the firm had returned half his fee. The false memory of his 'trip to Mars' hadn't taken – at least not entirely, not as he had been assured.

'Mr Quail,' the girl said, 'although you are a minor clerk you

21 'Christ': an exclamation of anger

are a good-looking man and it spoils your features to become angry. If it would make you feel any better, I might, ahem, let you take me out …'

He felt furious, then. 'I remember you,' he said savagely. 'For instance the fact that your breasts are sprayed blue; that stuck in my mind. And I remember Mr McClane's promise that if I remembered my visit to Rekal, Incorporated I'd receive my money back in full. Where is Mr McClane?'

After a delay – probably as long as they could manage – he found himself once more seated facing the imposing walnut desk, exactly as he had been an hour or so earlier in the day.

'Some technique you have,' Quail said sardonically. His disappointment – and resentment – was enormous, by now. 'My so-called "memory" of a trip to Mars as an undercover agent for Interplan is hazy and vague and shot full of contradictions. And I clearly remember my dealings here with you people. I ought to take this to the Better Business Bureau.' He was burning angry, at this point; his sense of being cheated had overwhelmed him, had destroyed his customary **aversion** to participating in a public **squabble**.

Looking **morose**, as well as cautious, McClane said, 'We capitulate, Quail. We'll refund the balance of your fee. I fully concede the fact that we did absolutely nothing for you.' His tone was resigned.

Quail said accusingly, 'You didn't even provide me with the various artifacts that you claimed would "prove" to me I had been on Mars. All that song-and-dance you went into – it hasn't materialized into a damn thing. Not even a ticket stub. Nor postcards. Nor passport. Nor proof of immunization shots. Nor – '

'Listen, Quail,' McClane said. 'Suppose I told you – ' He broke off. 'Let it go.' He pressed a button on his intercom. 'Shirley, will you disburse five hundred and seventy more 'creds in the form of a cashier's check[22] made out to Douglas Quail? Thank you.' He released the button, then glared at Quail.

Presently the check appeared; the receptionist placed it before McClane and once more vanished out of sight, leaving

22 US: British spelling is *cheque*

the two men alone, still facing each other across the surface of the massive walnut desk.

'Let me give you a word of advice,' McClane said as he signed the check and passed it over. 'Don't discuss your, ahem, recent trip to Mars with anyone.'

'What trip?'

'Well, that's the thing.' Doggedly, McClane said, 'The trip you partially remember. Act as if you don't remember; pretend it never took place. Don't ask me why; just take my advice: it'll be better for all of us.' He had begun to perspire. Freely. 'Now, Mr Quail, I have other business, other clients to see.' He rose, showed Quail to the door.

Quail said, as he opened the door, 'A firm that turns out such bad work shouldn't have any clients at all.' He shut the door behind him.

On the way home in the cab Quail pondered the wording of his letter of complaint to the Better Business Bureau, Terra Division. As soon as he could get to his typewriter he'd get started; it was clearly his duty to warn other people away from Rekal, Incorporated.

When he got back to his conapt he seated himself before his Hermes Rocket portable, opened the drawers and rummaged for carbon paper – and noticed a small, familiar box. A box which he had carefully filled on Mars with Martian fauna and later smuggled through customs.

Opening the box he saw, to his disbelief, six dead maw-worms and several varieties of the unicellular life on which the Martian worms fed. The protozoa[23] were dried-up, dusty, but he recognized them; it had taken him an entire day picking among the vast dark alien boulders to find them. A wonderful, illuminated journey of discovery.

But I didn't go to Mars, he realized.

Yet on the other hand –

Kirsten appeared at the doorway to the room, an armload of pale brown groceries gripped. 'Why are you home in the middle of the day?' her voice, in an eternity of sameness, was accusing.

23 very small living things made up of only one cell

'*Did I go to Mars?*' he asked her. 'You would know.'

'No, of course you didn't go to Mars; *you* would know that, I would think. Aren't you always bleating about going?'

He said, 'By God, I think I went.' After a pause, he added, 'And simultaneously I think I didn't go.'

'Make up your mind.'

'How can I?' He gestured. 'I have both memory-tracks grafted inside my head; one is real and one isn't but I can't tell which is which. Why can't I rely on you? They haven't **tinkered** with you.' She could do this much for him at least – even if she never did anything else.

Kirsten said in a level, controlled voice, 'Doug, if you don't pull yourself together, we're through. I'm going to leave you.'

'I'm in trouble.' His voice came out husky and coarse. And shaking. 'Probably I'm heading into a psychotic episode; I hope not, but – maybe that's it. It would explain everything, anyhow.'

Setting down the bag of groceries, Kristen **stalked** to the closet. 'I was not kidding,' she said to him quietly. She brought out a coat, got it on, walked back to the door of the conapt. 'I'll phone you one of these days soon,' she said tonelessly. 'This is goodbye, Doug. I hope you pull out of this eventually; I really pray you do. For your sake.'

'Wait,' he said desperately. 'Just tell me and make it absolute; I did go or I didn't – tell me which one.' *But they may have altered your memory-track also*, he realized.

The door closed. His wife had left. Finally!

A voice behind him said, 'Well, that's that. Now put up your hands, Quail. And also please turn around and face this way.'

He turned, instinctively, without raising his hands.

The man who faced him wore the plum uniform of the Interplan Police Agency, and his gun appeared to be UN issue. And, for some odd reason, he seemed familiar to Quail; familiar in a blurred, distorted fashion which he could not pin down. So, jerkily, he raised his hands.

'You remember,' the policeman said, 'your trip to Mars. We know all your actions today and all your thoughts – in particular your very important thoughts on the trip home from Rekal, Incorporated.' He explained, 'We have a tele-transmitter wired within your skull; it keeps us constantly informed.'

A telepathic transmitter; use of a living plasma that had been discovered on Luna. He shuddered with self-aversion. The thing lived inside him, within his own brain feeding, listening, feeding. But the Interplan police used them; that had come out even in the homeopapes. So this was probably true, dismal as it was.

'Why me?' Quail said huskily. What had he done – or thought? And what did this have to do with Rekal, Incorporated?

'Fundamentally,' the Interplan cop[24] said, 'this has nothing to do with Rekal; it's between you and us.' He tapped his right ear. 'I'm still picking up your mentational processes by the way of your cephalic transmitter.' In the man's ear Quail saw a small white-plastic plug. 'So I have to warn you: anything you think may be held against you.' He smiled. 'Not that it matters now; you've already thought and spoken yourself into oblivion. What's annoying is the fact that under narkidrine at Rekal, Incorporated you told them, their technicians and the owner, Mr McClane, about your trip – where you went, for whom, some of what you did. They're very frightened. They wish they had never laid eyes on you.' He added reflectively. 'They're right.'

Quail said, 'I never made any trip. It's false memory-chain improperly planted in me by McClane's technicians.' But then he thought of the box, in his desk drawer, containing the Martian life forms. And the trouble and hardship he had had gathering them. The memory seemed real. And the box of life forms; that certainly was real. Unless McClane had planted it. Perhaps this was one of the 'proofs' which McClane had talked **glibly** about.

The memory of my trip to Mars, he thought, *doesn't convince me – but unfortunately it has convinced the Interplan Police Agency. They think I really went to Mars and they think I at least partially realize it.*

'We not only know you went to Mars,' the Interplan cop agreed, in answer to his thoughts, 'but we know that you now remember enough to be difficult for us. And there's no use expunging your

24 *US, informal:* British word is *police officer*

conscious memory of all this, because if we do you'll simply show up at Rekal, Incorporated again and start over. And we can't do anything about McClane and his operation because we have no jurisdiction over anyone except our own people. Anyhow, McClane hasn't committed any crime.' He eyed Quail, 'Nor, technically, have you. You didn't go to Rekal, Incorporated with the idea of regaining your memory; you went, as we realize, for the usual reason people go there – a love by plain, dull people for adventure.' He added, 'Unfortunately you're not plain, not dull, and you've already had too much excitement; the last thing in the universe you needed was a course from Rekal, Incorporated. Nothing could have been more lethal for you or for us. And, for that matter, for McClane.'

Quail said, 'Why is it "difficult" for you if I remember my trip – my alleged trip – and what I did there?'

'Because,' the Interplan harness bull said, 'what you did is not in accord with our great white all-protecting father public image. You did, for us, what we never do. As you'll presently remember – thanks to narkidrine. That box of dead worms and algae has been sitting in your desk drawer for six months, ever since you got back. And at no time have you shown the slightest curiosity about it. We didn't even know you had it until you remembered it on your way home from Rekal; then we came here on the double to look for it.' He added, unnecessarily, 'Without any luck; there wasn't enough time.'

A second Interplan cop joined the first one; the two briefly conferred. Meanwhile, Quail thought rapidly. He did remember more, now; the cop had been right about narkidrine. They – Interplan – probably used it themselves. Probably? He knew darn well they did; he had seen them putting a prisoner on it. Where would *that* be? Somewhere on Terra? More likely on Luna, he decided, viewing the image rising from his highly defective – but rapidly less so – memory.

And he remembered something else. Their reason for sending him to Mars; the job he had done.

No wonder they had expunged[25] his memory.

25 *formal*: to remove something completely, especially from a written record

'Oh, God,' the first of the two Interplan cops said, breaking off his conversation with his companion. Obviously, he had picked up Quail's thoughts. 'Well, this is a far worse problem, now; as bad as it can get.' He walked toward Quail, again covering him with his gun. 'We've got to kill you,' he said. 'And right away.'

Nervously, his fellow officer said, 'Why right away? Can't we simply cart him off to Interplan New York and let them – '

'*He* knows why it has to be right away,' the first cop said; he too looked nervous, now, but Quail realized that it was for an entirely different reason. His memory had been brought back almost entirely, now. And he fully understood the officer's tension.

'On Mars,' Quail said hoarsely, 'I killed a man. After getting past fifteen bodyguards. Some armed with sneaky-pete guns, the way you are.' He had been trained, by Interplan, over a five year period to be an assassin. A professional killer. He knew ways to take out armed adversaries … such as these two officers; and the one with the ear-receiver knew it, too.

If he moved swiftly enough –

The gun fired. But he had already moved to one side, and at the same time he chopped down the gun-carrying officer. In an instant he had possession of the gun and was covering the other, confused, officer.

'Picked my thoughts up,' Quail said, panting for breath. 'He knew what I was going to do, but I did it anyhow.'

Half sitting up, the injured officer grated, 'He won't use that gun on you, Sam; I picked that up, too. He knows he's finished, and he knows we know it, too. Come on, Quail.' Laboriously, grunting with pain, he got shakily to his feet. He held out his hand. 'The gun,' he said to Quail. 'You can't use it, and if you turn it over to me I'll guarantee not to kill you; you'll be given a hearing, and someone higher up in Interplan will decide, not me. Maybe they can erase your memory once more, I don't know. But you know the thing I was going to kill you for; I couldn't keep you from remembering it. So my reason for wanting to kill you is in a sense past.'

Quail, clutching the gun, bolted from the conapt, **sprinted** for the elevator[26]. *If you follow me*, he thought, *I'll kill you. So don't.* He **jabbed** at the elevator button and, a moment later, the doors slid back.

The police hadn't followed him. Obviously they had picked up his terse, tense thoughts and had decided not to take the chance.

With him inside the elevator descended. He had gotten away – for a time. But what next? Where could he go?

The elevator reached the ground floor; a moment later Quail had joined the mob of peds[27] hurrying along the runnels. His head ached and he felt sick. But at least he had evaded death; they had come very close to shooting him on the spot, back in his own conapt.

And they probably will again, he decided. *When they find me. And with this transmitter inside me, that won't take too long.*

Ironically, he had gotten exactly what he had asked Rekal, Incorporated for. Adventure, peril, Interplan police at work, a secret and dangerous trip to Mars in which his life was at stake – everything he had wanted as a false memory.

The advantages of it being a memory – and nothing more – could now be appreciated.

5

On a park bench, alone, he sat dully watching a flock of perts: a semi-bird imported from Mars' two moons, capable of soaring flight, even against Earth's huge gravity.

Maybe I can find my way back to Mars, he pondered. But then what? It would be worse on Mars; the political organization whose leader he had assassinated would spot him the moment he stepped from the ship; he would have Interplan and *them* after him, there.

Can you hear me thinking? he wondered. Easy avenue to paranoia; sitting here alone he felt them tuning in on him,

26 US: British word is *lift*
27 pedestrians, people on foot

monitoring, recording discussing ... He shivered, rose to his feet, walked aimlessly, his hands deep in his pockets. *No matter where I go*, he realized, *you'll always be with me. As long as I have this device inside my head.*

I'll make a deal with you, he thought to himself – and to them. *Can you imprint a false-memory template on me again, as you did before, that I lived an average, routine life, never went to Mars? Never saw an Interplan uniform up close and never handled a gun?*

A voice inside his brain answered, 'As has been carefully explained to you: that would not be enough.'

Astonished, he halted.

'We formerly communicated with you in this manner,' the voice continued. 'When you were operating in the field, on Mars. It's been months since we've done it; we assumed, in fact, that we'd never have to do so again. Where are you?'

'Walking,' Quail said, 'to my death.' *By your officers' guns*, he added as an afterthought. 'How can you be sure it wouldn't be enough?' he demanded. 'Don't the Rekal techniques work?'

'As we said. If you're given a set of standard, average memories you get – restless. You'd inevitably seek out Rekal or one of its competitors again. We can't go through this a second time.'

'Suppose,' Quail said, 'once my authentic memories have been cancelled, something more vital than standard memories are implanted. Something which would act to satisfy my **craving**,' he said. 'That's been proved; that's probably why you initially hired me. But you ought to be able to come up with something else – something equal. I was the richest man on Terra but I finally gave all my money to educational foundations. Or I was a famous deep-space explorer. Anything of that sort; wouldn't one of those do?'

Silence.

'Try it,' he said desperately. 'Get some of your top-notch[28] military psychiatrists; explore my mind. Find out what my most expansive daydream is.' He tried to think. 'Women,' he said. 'Thousands of them, like Don Juan had. An interplanetary playboy – a mistress in every city on Earth, Luna and Mars. Only

28 *informal*: best

I gave that up, out of exhaustion. Please,' he begged. 'Try it.'

'You'd voluntarily surrender, then?' the voice inside his head asked. 'If we agreed, to arrange such a solution? *If it's possible?*'

After an interval of hesitation he said, 'Yes.' *I'll take the risk,* he said to himself, *that you don't simply kill me.*

'You make the first move,' the voice said presently. 'Turn yourself over to us. And we'll investigate that line of possibility. If we can't do it, however, if your authentic memories begin to crop up again as they've done at this time, then – ' There was silence and then the voice finished, 'We'll have to destroy you. As you must understand. Well, Quail, you still want to try?'

'Yes,' he said. Because the alternative was death now – and for certain. At least this way he had a chance, slim as it was.

'You present yourself at our main barracks in New York,' the voice of the Interplan cop resumed. 'At 580 Fifth Avenue, floor twelve. Once you've surrendered yourself, we'll have our psychiatrists begin on you; we'll have personality-profile tests made. We'll attempt to determine your absolute, ultimate fantasy wish – then we'll bring you back to Rekal, Incorporated, here; get them in on it, fulfilling that wish in vicarious[29] surrogate[30] retrospection[31]. And – good luck. We do owe you something; you acted as a capable instrument for us.' The voice lacked malice; if anything, they – the organization – felt sympathy toward him.

'Thanks,' Quail said. And began searching for a robot cab.

6

'Mr Quail' the stern-faced, elderly Interplan psychiatrist said, 'you possess a most interesting wish-fulfillment[32] dream fantasy. Probably nothing such as you consciously entertain or suppose. This is commonly the way; I hope it won't upset you too much to hear about it.'

The senior ranking Interplan officer present said briskly, 'He better not be too much upset to hear about it, not if he expects not to get shot.'

29 experienced through the actions of others
30 replacement
31 memory
32 *US spelling:* British spelling is *fulfilment*

'Unlike the fantasy of wanting to be an Interplan undercover agent,' the psychiatrist continued, 'which, being relatively speaking a product of maturity, had a certain plausibility to it, this production is a grotesque dream of your childhood; it is no wonder you fail to recall it. Your fantasy is this; you are nine years old, walking alone down a rustic lane. An unfamiliar variety of space vessel from another star system lands directly in front of you. No one on Earth but you, Mr Quail, sees it. The creatures within are very small and helpless, somewhat on the order of field mice, although they are attempting to invade Earth; tens of thousands of other ships will soon be on their way, when this advance party gives the go-ahead signal.'

'And I suppose I stop them,' Quail said, experiencing a mixture of amusement and disgust. 'Single-handed I **wipe them out**. Probably by stepping on them with my foot.'

'No,' the psychiatrist said patiently. 'You halt the invasion, but not by destroying them. Instead, you show them kindness and mercy, even though by telepathy – their mode of communication – you know why they have come. They have never seen such humane traits exhibited by any sentient[33] organism, and to show their appreciation they make a covenant[34] with you.'

Quail said. 'They won't invade Earth as long as I'm alive.'

'Exactly.' To the Interplan officer the psychiatrist said, 'You can see it does fit his personality, despite his **feigned scorn**.'

'So by merely existing,' Quail said, feeling a growing pleasure, 'by simply being alive, I keep Earth safe from alien rule. I'm in effect, then, the most important person on Terra. Without lifting a finger.'

'Yes, indeed, sir,' the psychiatrist said. 'And this is bedrock[35] in your psyche; this is a life-long childhood fantasy. Which, without depth and drug therapy, you never would have recalled. But it has always existed in you; it went underneath, but never ceased.'

33 *formal*: capable of feelings
34 agreement
35 fundamental

To McClane, who sat intently listening, the senior police official said, 'Can you implant an extra-factual memory pattern that extreme in him?'

'We get handed every possible type of wish-fantasy there is,' McClane said. 'Frankly, I've heard a lot worse than this. Certainly we can handle it. Twenty-four hours from now he won't just *wish* he'd saved Earth; he'll devoutly believe it really happened.'

The senior police official said, 'You can start the job, then. In preparation we've already once again erased the memory in him of his trip to Mars.'

Quail said, 'What trip to Mars?'

No one answered him, so reluctantly, he shelved the question. And anyhow a police vehicle had now put in its appearance; he, McClane, and the senior police officer crowded into it, and presently they were on their way to Chicago and Rekal, Incorporated.

'You had better make no errors this time,' the police officer said to heavy-set, nervous-looking McClane.

'I can't see what could go wrong,' McClane mumbled, perspiring. 'This has nothing to do with Mars or Interplan. Single-handedly stopping an invasion of Earth from another star-system.' He shook his head at that. 'Wow, what a kid dreams up. And by **pious** virtue, too; not by force. It's sort of **quaint**.' He dabbed at his forehead with a large linen pocket handkerchief.

Nobody said anything.

'In fact,' McClane said, 'it's touching.'

'But arrogant,' the police official said starkly. '**Inasmuch** as when he dies the invasion will resume. No wonder he doesn't recall it; it's the most grandiose fantasy I ever ran across.' He eyed Quail with disapproval. 'And to think we put this man on our payroll.'

When they reached Rekal, Incorporated the receptionist, Shirley, met them breathlessly in the outer office. 'Welcome back, Mr Quail,' she fluttered, her melon-shaped breasts – today painted an incandescent orange – bobbing with agitation. 'I'm sorry everything worked out so badly before; I'm sure this time it'll go better.'

Still repeatedly dabbing at his shiny forehead with his neatly folded Irish linen handkerchief, McClane said, 'It better.' Moving with rapidity he rounded up Lowe and Keeler, escorted them and Douglas Quail to the work area, and then, with Shirley and the senior police officer, returned to his familiar office. To wait.

'Do we have a packet made up for this, Mr McClane?' Shirley asked, bumping against him in her agitation, then coloring[36] modestly.

'I think we do.' He tried to recall, then gave up and consulted the formal charts. 'A combination,' he decided aloud, 'of packets Eighty-one, Twenty, and Six.' From the vault section of the chamber behind his desk he fished out the appropriate packets, carried them to his desk for inspection. 'From Eighty-one,' he explained, 'a magic healing rod given him – the client in question, this time Mr Quail – by the race of beings from another system. A token of their gratitude.'

'Does it work?' the police officer asked curiously.

'It did once,' McClane explained. 'But he, ahem, you see, used it up years ago, healing right and left. Now it's only a **memento**. But he remembers it working spectacularly.' He chuckled, then opened packet Twenty. 'Documents from the UN Secretary General thanking him for saving Earth; this isn't precisely appropriate, because part of Quail's fantasy is that no one knows of the invasion except himself, but for the sake of verisimilitude[37] we'll throw it in.' He inspected packet Six, then. What came from this? He couldn't recall; frowning; he dug into the plastic bag as Shirley and the Interplan police officer watched intently.

'Writing,' Shirley said. 'In a funny language.'

'This tells me who they were,' McClane said, 'and where they came from. Including a detailed star map logging their flight here and the system of origin. Of course it's in *their* script, so he can't read it. But he remembers them reading it to him in his

36 *US spelling:* British spelling is *colouring*
37 *formal:* the appearance of being real

own tongue.' He placed the **artifacts** in the center[38] of the desk. 'These should be taken to Quail's conapt,' he said to the police officer. 'So that when he gets home he'll find them. And it'll confirm his fantasy. SOP – standard operating procedure.' He chuckled apprehensively, wondering how matters were going with Lowe and Keeler.

The intercom buzzed. 'Mr McClane, I'm sorry to bother you.' It was Lowe's voice; he froze as he recognized it, froze and became mute. 'But something's come up. Maybe it would be better if you came in here and supervised. Like before, Quail reacted well to the narkidrine; he's unconscious, relaxed and receptive. But – '

McClane sprinted for the work area.

On a hygienic bed Douglas Quail lay breathing slowly and regularly, eyes half-shut, dimly conscious of those around him.

'We started interrogating him,' Lowe said, white-faced. 'To find out exactly when to place the fantasy-memory of him single-handedly having saved Earth. And strangely enough –'

'They told me not to tell,' Douglas Quail mumbled in a dull drug-saturated voice. 'That was the agreement. I wasn't even supposed to remember. But how could I forget an event like that?'

I guess it would be hard, McClane reflected. *But you did – until now.*

'They even gave me a scroll,' Quail mumbled, 'of gratitude, I have it hidden in my conapt; I'll show it to you.'

To the Interplan officer who had followed after him, McClane said, 'Well, I offer the suggestion that you better not kill him. If you do they'll return.'

'They also gave me a magic invisible destroying rod,' Quail mumbled, eyes totally shut now. 'That's how I killed that man on Mars you sent me to take out. It's in my drawer along with the box of Martian maw-worms and dried-up plant life.'

Wordlessly, the Interplan officer turned and stalked from the work area.

I might as well put those packets of proof-artifacts away, McClane said to himself resignedly. He walked, step by step, back to his

38 *US spelling:* British spelling is *centre*

office. *Including the citation from the UN Secretary General. After all –*

The real one probably would not be long in coming.

Post-reading exercises

Understanding the story

1 Use these questions to help you check that you have understood
   the story.

1

1 What is Quail's first thought when he wakes up?
2 Why can't he go to Mars?
3 How do you know he is not satisfied by his job?
4 What kind of relationship does he have with his wife?
5 What does she think of his obsession?
6 What alternative does she offer?

2

7 What is written on the sign Quail reads outside the building?
8 How does he feel as he approaches the building?
9 Why do Mr McClane's clothes reassure Quail?
10 In what way, according to McClane, is a false memory better than
   a real memory?
11 How does Quail feel as he is taken to the laboratory?

3

12 Are the objects in the packets real or imitations?
13 What is McClane going to do with them?
14 Why do the technicians call McClane?
15 Where is Quail?
16 Has the false memory already been implanted?
17 In what way is Quail different?
18 Why is he talking about Mars?
19 What can he remember?
20 Why is this a problem?
21 What does Quail suddenly understand about his wife?
22 Why might it be dangerous to implant a false memory on top of a
   real memory?
23 What does McClane decide to do? Why?

4

24 Where does Quail think he's just been?
25 What details does he remember?
26 Why does he put his hand in his pocket?
27 What does he find?

28 What effect does this have on his memory?

29 What does he tell his wife?

30 How does she react?

31 Why does she react like this?

32 Why does Quail go back to Rekal?

33 What does he think has happened?

34 What advice does McClane give Quail?

35 What does Quail find in his drawer?

36 Why does this confuse him?

37 What does he want his wife to tell him?

38 Why does his wife walk out on him?

39 Where do the Interplan police officers come from?

40 Why does the officer look familiar?

41 How does the policeman know what Quail is thinking?

42 Why are McClane and his technicians frightened?

43 Why can't Interplan simply remove Quail's memory of Mars?

44 Why is it important that no one knows what Quail did on Mars?

45 How does Quail escape from the flat?

5

46 Why can't Quail go back to Mars?

47 How does he communicate with the Interplan agents?

48 Why is his first suggestion not possible?

49 What is his second suggestion?

50 What are Quail's reasons for making the suggestion?

51 What are Interplan's reasons for accepting it?

6

52 What is Quail's fantasy?

53 How did he save the planet from invasion in his fantasy?

54 Why is he the most important person on Terra?

55 What do McClane and the police officer think of Quail's fantasy?

56 What objects does McClane choose to support Quail's fantasy?

57 Why do the technicians call McClane?

58 What has Quail remembered this time?

59 What advice does McClane offer the police officer? Why?

Language study

The concept of time and the sequence of events (what happened when) in the story is complex. This is reflected in the use of verbs in this story, and of the perfect aspect in particular. For example, take the concept being expressed here by McClane as he tries to persuade Quail of the advantages of a false memory:

> 'This is the only way you can achieve your, ahem, life-long dream; am I not correct, sir? You can't be this; you can't actually do this.' He chuckled. 'But you can **have been** and **have done**. We see to that.'

There are two contrasting realities here:

1 Quail **will not have been** to Mars in reality, BUT
2 He will remember **having been** to Mars.

Which are further confused by a third reality:

3 Quail **has** actually already **been** to Mars in real life.

Perfect aspect

Form

Perfect verb forms are formed using *have* + a past participle, eg *been, done*. The verb *have* can be in any tense or form, eg:

present: *have/has* + pp *It's **been** my lifelong ambition.*

past: *had* + pp *The door closed. His wife **had left**. Finally!*

future: *will have* + pp *I **won't have gone**, no matter what proofs you provide me with.*

other modals: *might/could/should* etc + *have* + pp *They may **have altered** your memory-track.*

infinitive: *to have* + pp *You want **to have gone** to Mars.*

-ing form: *having* + pp *You won't remember ever **having been** here.*

Use

The perfect aspect shows that an action happened (or is going to happen) **before** a given point in time.

Look at this example: *I've been to Mars.*

The time reference here is now, the present, the action of going to Mars happened some time before the present.

————————————————— X ————————————————— NOW
a trip to Mars

The perfect aspect does not tell us **when** it happened. The irony in the example above is that when Quail says this he genuinely doesn't know (or remember) exactly when it happened, just that it happened at some time in the past, or that he has a memory of it **having happened**.

1 Complete the extracts with the correct perfect form of the verbs in brackets.

1 I .... (change) my mind; I don't want to go home.
2 He found himself once more seated facing the imposing walnut desk, exactly as he .... (be) an hour or so earlier in the day.
3 Why can't I rely on you? They .... (tinker) with you.
4 His memory .... (be) brought back almost entirely, now.
5 They wish they .... (never lay) eyes on you.
6 Nothing .... (could be) more lethal for you or for us.
7 This is a life-long childhood fantasy. ... It .... (exist/always) in you.
8 This is a life-long childhood fantasy. Which, without depth and drug therapy, you never .... (would recall).

2 Answer these questions using a perfect form.

1 Why did Quail visit Rekal in the first place?

2 Why did he ask the taxi to turn round and go back to the Rekal offices?

3 Why did McClane give him his money back?

4 How did the Interplan police know what Quail was thinking?

5 What memory did Rekal try to implant the second time?

6 What happened at the end of the story?

Using adverbs of manner in dialogue

The story contains a lot of dialogue, which is important both for understanding what is happening and for understanding the feelings of the people speaking. The author often uses adverbs of manner to intensify and clarify the emotion behind the words or the tension in the situation.

Form

Adverbs of manner are usually formed by adding *-ly* to an adjective, eg nervous – nervously. When reporting direct speech the adverb comes directly **after** the reporting verb.

*'Our problem,' Lowe said **sharply**, 'is something quite different.'*

Use

They are used to explain how the words are said, in what tone and with what emotion.

3 Look at these extracts. Use the adverbs from the box to complete each extract below.

> curiously   desperately   encouragingly   nervously   patiently
> respectfully   savagely   tonelessly

1 'Mr Quail,' McClane said .... 'As you explained in your letter to us, you have no chance, no possibility in the slightest, of ever actually getting to Mars; you can't afford it.'
2 'And our fee is reasonable; no hidden charges.' He smiled ....
3 'Recall what, sir or madam?' the robot driver of the cab inquired
   ....
4 'Oh, hello, Mr Quail,' she said .... 'H-how are you? Did you forget something?'
5 He felt furious, then. 'I remember you,' he said ....
6 'I'll phone you one of these days soon,' she said ....
7 'Wait,' he said .... 'Just tell me and make it absolute; I did go or I didn't – tell me which one.'
8 'Does it work?' the police officer asked ....

4 Look at the extracts again. What do the adverbs tell us about:

a) how the words were said?
b) the person who is speaking?

5 Dick uses particular adverbs of speech, to express very specific and complex emotions. Look at the adverbs in bold below. Match them to their definitions (a) to (f).

1 Kirsten to Quail first thing in the morning:
   *'Are you getting up or not?' his wife Kirsten asked **drowsily**.*
2 Kirsten to Quail, commenting on his dream:
   *'I'll bet it had to do with some women,' Kirsten said **witheringly**.*

3 Quail to McClane on his first visit to Rekal:
'*What do you want now?*' Quail said **harshly**. '*You've broken my cover. Get out of here before I take you all apart.*'

4 McClane to his technician, Lowe:
'*No,*' McClane said. '*And we're going to return half his fee.*'
'"*Half*"*! Why half?*'
McClane said **lamely**, '*It seems to be a good compromise.*'

5 Quail to McClane when he goes back to complain:
'*Some technique you have,*' Quail said **sardonically**. *His disappointment – and resentment – was enormous, by now.*

6 Interplan officer, discussing Quail's childhood fantasy:
'*But arrogant,*' the police official said **starkly**. '*Inasmuch as when he dies the invasion will resume.*'

a) only half awake
b) in a hard, unpleasant voice that expresses anger or impatience
c) with no respect or affection, and in a way that makes the person you're talking to feel silly or embarrassed
d) very simply and coldly, with no sympathy
e) in a way that does not seem sincere or enthusiastic
f) saying the opposite of what you mean in a way that shows a lack of respect for what someone else has said or done

6 Use the adverbs from the box to complete the sentences below.

1 'I'm sure you're doing your best!' she replied ....
2 'Goodnight,' she said .... as she turned over and went to sleep.
3 'He's dead,' the officer said .... He felt no need to express any emotion.
4 'I don't know. It just is,' he answered ....
5 'Don't you dare come anywhere near him. You've done enough damage already,' he said ....
6 'I don't suppose you remembered to put petrol in the car, did you?' she asked ....

Literary analysis

Plot

1 Order these events in sequence starting from the earliest;

Quail visited Rekal to get a memory implant of a trip to Mars_____
Quail visited Mars as a government secret agent _____
Quail saved the planet from invasion by aliens _____
Quail visited Rekal to get a memory implant of a meeting
with aliens when he was a child _____
Quail remembered meeting the aliens _____
Quail was trained as a government assassin _____
Quail's memory of his trip to Mars was erased _____
Quail's memory of his trip to Mars came back to him _____
Quail's memory of his meeting with the aliens was erased _____

2 Which of these events didn't actually happen?
3 Which do you think was the most important event? Why?
4 Who was responsible for erasing Quail's memories? Why were they
erased? How did he get them back again?
5 Can we be sure that Quail's childhood memory is true and not just
a fantasy?
6 What does the story tell us about the nature of memories and the
relationship between memories and reality?

Character

7 Who is the main character? What do you know about him? Give a
brief description of him.
8 What does Quail know about himself:
a) at the beginning of the story?
b) after his meeting with the Interplan agents in his flat?
c) at the end of the story?
9 In what way does Quail change during the story? How many
different Douglas Quails do we see?
10 Quail is both ordinary and heroic at the same time. In what ways is
Quail a hero? In what ways is he just an ordinary man?
11 Think about the other characters in the story. What does Quail
represent for:
a) McClane
b) Quail's wife, Kirsten
c) the Interplan agents?

12 What do you know about Quail's wife? What kind of woman is she? What is their marriage like? Is she really his wife? Does she know anything about his trip to Mars? Why does she leave him?

Narration

13 Who tells the story? From whose point of view is it told? What effect does this have on our perceptions of the main events?
14 The events are not described in the order they happened. Why not?
15 Look back at the list of main events in question 1 and order them according to the sequence in which we find out about them in the story.
16 Think about how the sequence increaes our suspense as each layer of memory is pulled back to reveal another layer of truth.
17 How predictable is the ending? When did you first suspect that Quail's fantasy might actually prove to be true? When it was first mentioned? When Lowe calls McClane on the intercom? When Quail starts to talk about his childhood experience under the influence of the narkidrine?

Style

18 Dick often uses short or unfinished sentences in his narrative. Look at these examples in the opening paragraph:

He awoke – and wanted Mars. **The valleys, he thought.** *What would it be like to trudge among them? Great and greater yet: the dream grew as he became fully conscious, the dream and the yearning. He could almost feel the enveloping presence of the other world, which only Government agents and high officials had seen.* **A clerk like himself? Not likely.**

What effect do they create? How do they help us enter the mind and viewpoint of Quail?

19 Look at some more examples. Notice the way Dick finishes each extract. What is the effect of this last detail, and the way it is given?

'Yes,' he said, and gazed out the kitchen window at the hovercars and traffic runnels, and all the little energetic people hurrying to work. In a little while he would be among them. ***As always.***

This was very different; what he did now was something else. Something which sooner or later had to happen.

*Was this the answer? After all, an illusion, no matter how convincing, remained nothing more than an illusion. At least objectively. But subjectively – **quite the opposite entirely.***

*The door closed. His wife had left. **Finally!***

20   The last extract shows another characteristic of Dick's style: the one-line paragraph. His story is punctuated by telegraphic paragraphs like the one above. A few, very simple words that tell a whole story.

21   Look at some more one-line paragraphs:
     He would have to wait and find out. [Page 25]
     He turned, instinctively, without raising his hands. [Page 34]
     No wonder they had expunged his memory. [Page 36]
     The advantages of it being a memory – and nothing more – could now be appreciated. [Page 38]
     McClane sprinted for the work area. [Page 44]
     The real one probably would not be long in coming. [Page 45]

22   Look at these paragraphs in the context of the story.
     –   What are they telling us about the story, or the characters?
     –   How do they add to the suspense?

Guidance to the above literary terms, answer keys to all the exercises and activities, plus a wealth of other reading-practice material, can be found on the student's section of the Macmillan Readers website at: www.macmillanenglish.com/readers.

A Sound of Thunder

by Ray Bradbury

About the author

Ray Douglas Bradbury is a US writer of fantasy, horror, science fiction and mystery. He is best known for his *Martian Chronicles*, and is widely considered to be one of the 20th century's greatest and most popular writers of science fiction. His works have been translated into more than 40 languages and have sold tens of millions of copies around the world. His popularity continues in the 21st century.

Bradbury was born in Illinois in August 1920. The family spent some time in Tucson, Arizona, but eventually settled in Los Angeles in 1934. Bradbury finished school in 1938 and chose not to go to college; instead he spent the next four years selling newspapers in the street and educating himself at the local library (which is the setting for one of his novels, *Something Wicked This Way Comes*). He also started writing science-fiction stories for science-fiction fanzines[1].

In 1941, at the age of twenty one, he published his first paid work, a short story called 'Pendulum', in the magazine *Super Science Stories*, and became a full-time writer. His first book, *Dark Carnival*, a collection of short stories, was published in 1947. In the same year, he married Marguerite McClure. The marriage was to last 50 years, until her death in 2003. They had four daughters and eight grandchildren.

During his long writing career, Bradbury has written almost 600 short stories, eleven novels, as well as various poems and plays. He has also written children's fiction as well as screenplays for film and TV. Many of Bradbury's stories and novels have been adapted for the cinema, radio, TV, theatre and comic books.

He first became famous for his *Martian Chronicles*, a short-story collection published in 1950. These early science stories were based on ancient Greek and Roman mythology. This was closely followed in 1953 by his best-known work, the short novel *Fahrenheit 451*, which describes a future where all books are restricted, and critical thought is against the law. The main character is a *fireman* (a book burner) and

---

1 Non-professional publications produced by fans of science fiction for the pleasure of others who share their interest

the title of the book refers to the temperature at which paper burns.

In 1946 Bradbury published a short story called 'Homecoming' in the Halloween issue of the *New Yorker*. It told the story of a strange family called the Elliotts. It was the first in a long series of stories about the same family that he wrote with his friend, Charles Addams. The series later became famous as *The Addams Family*.

Bradbury has won countless awards. In 2004 he was awarded the National Medal of Arts[2] by President George W Bush. He has also received the World Fantasy Award, an international award for outstanding achievement in the field of fantasy, and the Science Fiction Writers of America Grand Master Award for his lifetime's achievements. He has a star on the Hollywood Walk of Fame, an asteroid has been named in his honour (9766 Bradbury) and a crater on the moon was called 'Dandelion Crater' after his novel, *Dandelion Wine*.

Interestingly, he has little interest in, or love for, machines. He has never owned a car or learned to drive and he is afraid of flying.

About the story

The story was first published in *Collier's Magazine* in 1952. It was reprinted in various collections, most recently in *A Sound of Thunder and Other Stories* (2005). It is said to be the number one most republished science-fiction story[3].

The story has been adapted to comic form, and a film released in 2005 continues the story. A video game of the same name, based more closely on the film than the short story, was released in 2004.

The story is set in the USA in 2055. Time travel has become possible by means of a time machine. A company called Time Safari arranges hunting trips back in time, where the clients can shoot and kill prehistoric animals such as the Tyrannosaurus Rex.

Background information

Tyrannosaurus Rex

The first Tyrannosaurus Rex skeleton was found in 1892 in North America. The president of the American Museum of National History at the time, Henry Fairfield Osborne, gave it its name in 1905. The

2 An award created by the Congress of the USA in 1984. It is the highest honour that can be awarded to an individual on behalf of the people of the USA.

3 According to a *Locus Magazine* index to *Science Fiction Anthologies and Collections*.

name comes from the Greek words *tyrannos*, meaning tyrant, and *sauros*, which means lizard, and the Latin word *rex*, which means king.

The Tyrannosaurus Rex is definitely the most well-known of all the dinosaurs. It was also one of the largest meat-eating animals of all time. It lived in the late Cretaceous period, about 86 to 65 million years ago. It lived in humid, semi-tropical swamps[4] and forests.

Tyrannosaurus Rex was about 12 metres long and 6 metres tall. It weighed approximately 6 tons. It had an enormous head with large pointed teeth in its gigantic jaws[5]. It had huge hind legs, but very small arms, which were no more than 1 metre long. Its hands had two fingers, each with a large hard claw. It had a stiff, pointed tail that counterbalanced the weight of its head and helped it to turn quickly when running. Its body was solid but its bones were hollow[6] like those of a bird. Its skin was scaly, like that of an alligator.

Bradbury's description of the dinosaur in his story remains totally faithful to the scientific evidence and knowledge available in his day.

The Butterfly Effect

'The Butterfly Effect' is a theory that explores the nature of cause and effect. It is summarised in the image of a butterfly flapping its wings on one side of the world and creating a tornado on the other side. It does not suggest that this consequence has to happen. Quite the opposite, it suggests that there are a number of possible situations that could follow as a result of that simple movement. The movement of the butterfly's wings does not cause the tornado as such, but movement or change in atmosphere as small as that of the flapping of a butterfly's wings can influence the time and place of the tornado's occurrence.

It is probable that the theory of the Butterfly Effect took its name from Bradbury's story, although in A *Sound of Thunder* Bradbury is looking not at weather, but at time and the evolution of history. When it was first published in 1961 (nine years after Bradbury's story), the researcher Edward Lorenz referred to a seagull rather than a butterfly, but in later speeches and papers he replaced the seagull with the butterfly.

---

4 an area of land covered by water where trees and plants grow
5 the part of your mouth where your teeth grow
6 empty in the middle

Time paradox

According to the theory of the Butterfly Effect, the very fact of being able to travel back in time will change the future. The simple presence of the time travellers will affect short-term events, no matter how careful they are. This means that anyone who travels into the past will change the future and will never actually be able to return to the same reality that they came from.

Summary

It may help you to know something about what happens in the story before you read it. Don't worry, this summary does *not* tell you how the story ends!

Eckels is a hunter. He has hunted all kinds of wild animals on various safaris but now he wants to travel back in time to hunt a Tyrannosaurus Rex. Time Safari Inc. is a company that organises safaris in the past. They have a time machine that can take hunters back in time to shoot any animal they want.

Eckels arrives at Time Safari. He is introduced to his guide, Mr Travis. He is a little nervous and very impressed by the time machine. Before he pays the $10,000 for the safari, the man at the desk reminds him of how dangerous dinosaur hunting can be.

They enter the time machine and begin to travel back in time. There are five people in the machine in total, two guides and three hunters. They talk about how to kill a dinosaur. The machine arrives at its destination.

The guide explains the rules of the safari and insists on the importance of staying on the path and not touching or disturbing any of the wildlife around them. He explains that the tyrannosaurus they are going to hunt that day has been chosen specially for the hunt and that they are not to shoot at or kill any other animals.

They leave the machine and enter the prehistoric jungle with its strange sights and sounds. Eckels is very nervous at the idea of shooting a tyrannosaurus and when the animal finally appears he panics. He can't shoot, he turns around and, confused and frightened, walks off the path and into the jungle.

The others continue with the hunt and kill the tyrannosaurus as planned. When they get back to the time machine, Eckels is waiting for them. Now it is time for them to travel back to the future.

Pre-reading exercises

Key vocabulary

This section will help you familiarise yourself with some of the more specific vocabulary used in the story. You may want to use it to help you before you start reading, or as a revision exercise after you have finished the story.

Hunting

The subject of the story is a prehistoric safari and the story contains some specific vocabulary associated with hunting.

1 **Look at the words in bold in the sentences below and match them to their definitions (a) to (k).**

1 *We're here to give you the severest thrill a real hunter ever asked for. Traveling[7] you back sixty million years to **bag** the biggest **game** in all of Time.*

2 *I **track** them through their entire existence, noting which of them lives longest.*

3 *Eckels, balanced on the narrow Path, **aimed** his rifle playfully.*

4 *'Stop that!' said Travis. 'Don't even aim for fun, blast you[8]! If your guns should **go off**–'*

5 *He heard Travis shift his **rifle**, click the **safety catch**, and raise the weapon.*

6 *Put your first two **shots** into the eyes, if you can, blind them, and go back into the brain.*

7 *The rifle in his hands seemed a **cap gun**. 'We were fools to come. This is impossible.*

8 *They **fired** at the metallic eyelids and the blazing black iris.*

9 *We can't take a **trophy** back to the Future. The body has to stay right here where it would have died originally.*

---

7 *US spelling:* British spelling is *travelling*
8 *informal:* used for showing you are angry

(a) to point a gun at something you want to shoot
(b) to catch and kill an animal you are hunting
(c) a toy gun
(d) to shoot at something
(e) animals or birds that you catch when you hunt
(f) to shoot a gun accidentally
(g) a large gun with a long barrel that you hold against your shoulder when you shoot
(h) the part of a gun that stops you from accidentally shooting with it
(i) the bullet which comes out of the gun and hits something
(j) to follow or find an animal
(k) something that you keep as proof of an achievement you are proud of, for example a part of an animal you have killed

2 Use the words in bold above to complete these sentences.

1 The biggest.................he had ever....................was an elephant. He had cut off and kept one of its feet as a ....

2 He forgot to put the .... on and the gun .... as he was cleaning it.

3 He carefully .... his .... at the bottle, took a deep breath and .... The bottle fell to the ground in a thousand pieces.

4 He .... the deer through the forest, being careful not to be seen.

Nervous movements

Eckels, the main character in the story, is excited about the idea of hunting a Tyrannosaurus Rex. His movements often show how nervous he is.

3 Look at the verbs and their definitions. Then use them to complete the sentences below. Sometimes more than one verb is possible.

flush if someone flushes, their face becomes red because they are hot or ill, or are feeling angry, embarrassed, or excited
fumble to try to hold, move, or find something using your hands in a way that is not skilful or graceful
scrabble to make a lot of small quick movements with your fingers, especially when you are trying to find something you can't see
shiver if you shiver, your body shakes slightly, for example because you are cold or frightened

> **shuffle** to walk slowly without lifting your feet or to keep moving your feet because you are nervous, embarrassed or bored
> **stiffen** to suddenly hold your body in a stiff (rigid) way
> **sway** to move gently from side to side
> **tremble** if your body or part of your body trembles, it shakes, usually because you are nervous, afraid or excited
> **twitch** to make a sudden short movement

1 His face .... bright red when Travis shouted at him.

2 Eckels .... blindly in his pocket for his cheque book.

3 He .... desperately at the mud on his shoes, trying to get it off.

4 He sat on the floor .... violently. Fear had taken control of his body.

5 He wrapped his arms around his knees and started to .... gently from side to side.

6 He .... off along the path, not really knowing where he was going or what he was doing.

7 His back .... suddenly. He had heard a strange noise. He turned round to see what it was.

8 His hand .... once or twice as he reached out for his gun.

Main themes

Before you read the story, you may want to think about some of the main themes that come up. The questions will help you think about the story as you are reading it for the first time. There is more discussion of the main themes in the *Literary analysis* section after the story.

Unseen consequences

The story explores the way a seemingly unimportant event can have far-reaching and significant consequences.

4 As you read the story answer these questions:

a) What precautions does the Time Safari company take to minimise its effects on the past? Why do they take so many precautions?

b) Is it possible to visit somewhere and not have any effect on it? Think also about how man's presence affects remote areas on the planet.

Time travel

Time travel is a recurring theme in science fiction. It is used to explore the relationship between past, present and future.

5 As you read, think about these questions:

a) What kind of future world does Bradbury imagine?

b) Is it very different from our own world today?

c) Was it very different from the world Bradbury lived in at the time the story was written?

d) What alternative society does he show us at the end? In what way is it different from the world the time travellers left behind?

A Sound of Thunder

by Ray Bradbury

1

The sign on the wall seemed to **quaver** under a film of sliding warm water. Eckels felt his eyelids blink over his stare, and the sign burned in this momentary darkness:

> TIME SAFARI, INC.
> SAFARIS TO ANY YEAR IN THE PAST.
> YOU NAME THE ANIMAL.
> WE TAKE YOU THERE.
> YOU SHOOT IT.

A warm phlegm gathered in Eckels' throat; he swallowed and pushed it down. The muscles around his mouth formed a smile as he put his hand slowly out upon the air, and in that hand waved a check[9] for ten thousand dollars to the man behind the desk.

"Does this safari guarantee I come back alive?"

"We guarantee nothing," said the official, "except the dinosaurs." He turned. "This is Mr Travis, your Safari Guide in the Past. He'll tell you what and where to shoot. If he says no shooting, no shooting. If you disobey instructions, there's a stiff penalty of another ten thousand dollars, plus possible government action, on your return."

Eckels glanced across the vast office at a mass and **tangle**, a snaking and humming of wires and steel boxes, at an **aurora** that **flickered** now orange, now silver, now blue. There was a sound like a gigantic **bonfire** burning all of Time, all the years and all the parchment calendars, all the hours piled high and set **aflame**.

9 *US spelling*: British spelling is *cheque*

A touch of the hand and this burning would, on the instant, beautifully reverse itself. Eckels remembered the wording in the advertisements to the letter. Out of chars[10] and ashes, out of dust and coals, like golden salamanders[11], the old years, the green years, might leap; roses sweeten the air, white hair turn Irish-black, wrinkles vanish; all, everything fly back to seed, flee death, rush down to their beginnings, suns rise in western skies and set in glorious easts, moons eat themselves opposite to the custom, all and everything cupping one in another like Chinese boxes, rabbits into hats, all and everything returning to the fresh death, the seed death, the green death, to the time before the beginning. A touch of a hand might do it, the merest touch of a hand.

"Unbelievable." Eckels breathed, the light of the Machine on his thin face. "A real Time Machine." He shook his head. "Makes you think. If the election had gone badly yesterday, I might be here now running away from the results. Thank God Keith won. He'll make a fine President of the United States."

"Yes," said the man behind the desk. "We're lucky. If Deutscher had gotten[12] in, we'd have the worst kind of dictatorship. There's an anti-everything man for you, a militarist, anti-Christ, anti-human, anti-intellectual. People called us up, you know, joking but not joking. Said if Deutscher became President they wanted to go live in 1492[13]. Of course it's not our business to conduct Escapes, but to form Safaris. Anyway, Keith's President now. All you got to worry about is –"

"Shooting my dinosaur," Eckels finished it for him.

"A *Tyrannosaurus rex*. The Tyrant Lizard, the most incredible monster in history. Sign this release[14]. Anything happens to you, we're not responsible. Those dinosaurs are hungry."

Eckels flushed angrily. "Trying to scare me!"

"Frankly, yes. We don't want anyone going who'll panic at the first shot. Six Safari leaders were killed last year, and a dozen

10 the blackened remains of a fire
11 a small animal, similar to a lizard that lives both on land and in water
12 US: past participle of *get*
13 The year Christopher Columbus first landed on the American continent.
14 An insurance document which states that the client will take full responsibility for their actions and any damage they may suffer or cause

hunters. We're here to give you the severest **thrill** a *real* hunter ever asked for. Traveling[15] you back sixty million years to bag the biggest game in all of Time. Your personal check's still there. Tear it up."

Mr Eckels looked at the check. His fingers twitched.

"Good luck," said the man behind the desk. "Mr Travis, he's all yours."

They moved silently across the room, taking their guns with them, toward the Machine, toward the silver metal and the roaring light.

2

First a day and then a night and then a day and then a night, then it was day-night-day-night-day. A week, a month, a year, a decade! A.D. 2055 A.D. 2019. 1999! 1957! Gone! The Machine roared.

They put on their oxygen helmets and tested the intercoms.

Eckels swayed on the padded seat, his face pale, his jaw stiff. He felt the trembling in his arms and he looked down and found his hands tight on the new rifle. There were four other men in the Machine. Travis, the Safari Leader, his assistant, Lesperance, and two other hunters, Billings and Kramer. They sat looking at each other, and the years blazed around them.

"Can these guns get a dinosaur cold?" Eckels felt his mouth saying.

"If you hit them right," said Travis on the helmet radio. "Some dinosaurs have two brains, one in the head, another far down the spinal column. We stay away from those. That's stretching luck. Put your first two shots into the eyes, if you can, blind them, and go back into the brain."

The Machine **howled**. Time was a film run backward. Suns fled and ten million moons fled after them. "Think," said Eckels. "Every hunter that ever lived would envy us today. This makes Africa seem like Illinois."

The Machine slowed; its scream fell to a murmur. The Machine stopped.

15 *US spelling*: British spelling is *travelling*

The sun stopped in the sky.

The fog that had **enveloped** the Machine blew away and they were in an old time, a very old time indeed, three hunters and two Safari Heads with their blue metal guns across their knees.

"Christ isn't born yet," said Travis. "Moses has not gone to the mountain to talk with God. The Pyramids are still in the earth, waiting to be cut out and put up. *Remember* that. Alexander, Caesar, Napoleon, Hitler – none of them exists."

The men nodded.

"That"– Mr. Travis pointed – "is the jungle of sixty million two thousand and fifty-five years before President Keith."

He indicated a metal path that struck off into green wilderness, over steaming **swamp**, among giant ferns and palms.

"And that," he said, "is the Path, laid by Time Safari for your use. It floats six inches above the earth. Doesn't touch so much as one grass blade, flower, or tree. It's an anti-gravity metal. Its purpose is to keep you from touching this world of the past in any way. Stay on the Path. Don't go off it. I repeat. *Don't go off.* For *any* reason! If you fall off, there's a penalty. And don't shoot any animals we don't okay."

"Why?" asked Eckels.

They sat in the ancient wilderness. Far birds' cries blew on a wind, and the smell of **tar** and old salt sea, moist grasses, and flowers the color[16] of blood.

"We don't want to change the Future. We don't belong here in the Past. The government doesn't *like* us here. We have to pay big graft[17] to keep our franchise. A Time Machine is finicky[18] business. Not knowing it, we might kill an important animal, a small bird, a roach[19], a flower even, thus destroying an important **link** in a growing species."

"That's not clear," said Eckels.

"All right," Travis continued, "say we accidentally kill one mouse here. That means all the future families of this one particular mouse are destroyed, right?"

16 US *spelling:* British spelling is *colour*
17 *informal, idiom:* a lot of money
18 more complicated than necessary and difficult to deal with
19 US: British is a *cockroach*, an insect similar to a beetle that lives in places where food is kept

"Right."

"And all the families of the families of the families of that one mouse! With a stamp of your foot, you **annihilate** first one, then a dozen, then a thousand, a million, a *billion* possible mice!"

"So they're dead," said Eckels. "So what?"

"So what?" Travis **snorted** quietly. "Well, what about the foxes that'll need those mice to survive? For want of ten mice, a fox dies. For want of ten foxes, a lion starves. For want of a lion, all manner of insects, vultures, infinite billions of life forms are thrown into chaos and destruction. Eventually it all boils down to this: fifty-nine million years later, a caveman, one of a dozen of the *entire world*, goes hunting **wild boar**, or saber-toothed tiger for food. But you, friend, have *stepped* on all the tigers in that region. By stepping on *one* single mouse. So the caveman starves. And the caveman, please note, is not just *any* expendable man, no! He is an *entire future nation*. From his loins[20] would have sprung ten sons. From *their loins* one hundred sons, and thus onward to a civilization. Destroy this one man, and you destroy a race, a people, an entire history of life. It is comparable to **slaying** some of Adam[21]'s grandchildren. The **stomp** of your foot, on one mouse, could start an earthquake, the effects of which could shake our earth and destinies down through Time, to their very foundations. With the death of that one caveman, a billion others yet unborn are throttled[22] in the womb. Perhaps Rome never rises on its seven hills. Perhaps Europe is forever a dark forest, and only Asia waxes[23] healthy and **teeming**. Step on a mouse and you **crush** the Pyramids. Step on a mouse and you leave your print, like a Grand Canyon, across Eternity. Queen Elizabeth might never be born. Washington might not cross the Delaware[24], there might never be a United States at all. So be careful. Stay on the Path. *Never* step off!"

"I see," said Eckels. "Then it wouldn't pay for us even to touch the *grass*?"

20 *mainly literary*: the sex organs
21 the first man according to the Bible
22 to kill someone or something by squeezing their throat so that they cannot breathe
23 *mainly literary*: to become bigger or stronger
24 a famous attack during the US Revolution

"Correct. Crushing certain plants could add up infinitesimally. A little error here would multiply in sixty million years, all out of proportion. Of course maybe our theory is wrong. Maybe Time *can't* be changed by us. Or maybe it can be changed only in little subtle ways. A dead mouse here makes an insect imbalance there, a population disproportion later, a bad harvest further on, a depression, mass starvation, and, finally, a change in *social* temperament in far-flung countries. Something much more subtle, like that. Perhaps only a soft breath, a whisper, a hair, pollen on the air, such a slight, slight change that unless you looked close you wouldn't see it. Who knows? Who really can say he knows? We don't know. We're guessing. But until we do know for certain whether our messing around in Time *can* make a big roar or a little rustle in history, we're being careful. This Machine, this Path, your clothing and bodies, were sterilized, as you know, before the journey. We wear these oxygen helmets so we can't introduce our bacteria into an ancient atmosphere."

"How do we know which animals to shoot?"

"They're marked with red paint," said Travis. "Today, before our journey, we sent Lesperance here back with the Machine. He came to this particular era and followed certain animals."

"Studying them?"

"Right," said Lesperance. "I track them through their entire existence, noting which of them lives longest. Very few. How many times they **mate**. Not often. Life's short. When I find one that's going to die when a tree falls on him, or one that drowns in a **tar pit**, I note the exact hour, minute, and second. I shoot a paint bomb. It leaves a red patch on his side. We can't miss it. Then I correlate our arrival in the Past so that we meet the Monster not more than two minutes before he would have died anyway. This way, we kill only animals with no future, that are never going to mate again. You see how *careful* we are?"

"But if you came back this morning in Time," said Eckels eagerly, "you must've bumped into *us*, our Safari! How did it turn out? Was it successful? Did all of us get through – alive?"

Travis and Lesperance gave each other a look.

"That'd be a paradox[25]," said the latter. "Time doesn't permit that sort of mess – a man meeting himself. When such occasions threaten, Time steps aside. Like an airplane hitting an air pocket. You felt the Machine jump just before we stopped? That was us passing ourselves on the way back to the Future. We saw nothing. There's no way of telling *if* this expedition was a success, *if we* got our monster, or whether all of us – meaning *you*, Mr Eckels – got out alive."

Eckels smiled palely.

"Cut that," said Travis sharply. "Everyone on his feet!"

They were ready to leave the Machine.

The jungle was high and the jungle was broad and the jungle was the entire world forever and forever. Sounds like music and sounds like flying tents filled the sky, and those were pterodactyls[26] soaring with **cavernous** gray[27] wings, gigantic bats of delirium and night fever. Eckels, balanced on the narrow Path, aimed his rifle playfully.

"Stop that!" said Travis. "Don't even aim for fun, blast you[28]! If your guns should go off – "

Eckels flushed. "Where's our *Tyrannosaurus*?"

Lesperance checked his wristwatch. "Up ahead. We'll bisect his trail in sixty seconds. Look for the red paint! Don't shoot till we give the word. Stay on the path. *Stay on the Path!*"

They moved forward in the wind of morning.

"Strange," murmured Eckels. "Up ahead, sixty million years, Election Day over. Keith made President. Everyone celebrating. And here we are, a million years lost, and they don't exist. The things we worried about for months, a lifetime, not even born or thought of yet."

"Safety catches off, everyone!" ordered Travis. "You, first shot, Eckels. Second, Billings. Third, Kramer."

"I've hunted tiger, wild boar, buffalo, elephant, but now, this is *it*," said Eckels. "I'm shaking like a kid."

25 a situation where two opposite and exclusive realities exist together at the same time
26 flying reptiles
27 US *spelling*: British spelling is *grey*
28 *informal, exclamation 'blast you!'*: used for showing you are angry

"Ah," said Travis.

Everyone stopped.

Travis raised his hand. "Ahead," he whispered. "In the mist. There he is. There's His Royal Majesty now."

The jungle was wide and full of twitterings, rustlings, murmurs, and sighs.

Suddenly it all ceased, as if someone had shut a door.

Silence.

A sound of thunder.

Out of the mist, one hundred yards away, came *Tyrannosaurus rex*.

"It," whispered Eckels. "It …"

"Sh!"

It came on great oiled, **resilient**, striding legs. It towered thirty feet above half of the trees, a great evil god, folding its delicate watchmaker's claws close to its oily reptilian chest. Each lower leg was a piston, a thousand pounds of white bone, sunk in thick ropes of muscle, sheathed over in a gleam of pebbled skin like the mail of a terrible warrior. Each thigh was a ton of meat, ivory, and steel mesh. And from the great breathing cage of the upper body those two delicate arms dangled out front, arms with hands which might pick up and examine men like toys, while the snake neck coiled. And the head itself, a ton of sculptured stone, lifted easily upon the sky. Its mouth gaped, exposing a fence of teeth like daggers. Its eyes rolled, ostrich eggs, empty of all expression save hunger. It closed its mouth in a death grin. It ran, its pelvic bones crushing aside trees and bushes, its taloned feet clawing damp earth, leaving prints six inches deep wherever it **settled** its weight. It ran with a gliding ballet step, far too **poised** and balanced for its ten tons. It moved into a sunlit arena warily, its beautifully reptilian hands feeling the air.

"Why, why," Eckels twitched his mouth. "It could reach up and grab the moon."

"Sh!" Travis jerked angrily. "He hasn't seen us yet."

"It can't be killed." Eckels pronounced his verdict quietly, as if there could be no argument. He had weighed the evidence and this was his considered opinion. The rifle in his hands seemed a cap gun. "We were fools to come. This is impossible."

"Shut up!" hissed Travis.

"Nightmare."

"Turn around," commanded Travis. "Walk quietly to the Machine. We'll **remit** one half of your fee."

"I didn't realize it would be this *big*," said Eckels. "I miscalculated, that's all. And now I want out."

"It *sees* us!"

"There's red paint on its chest!"

The Tyrant Lizard raised itself. Its armoured flesh glittered like a thousand green coins. The coins, crusted with slime, steamed. In the slime, tiny insects wriggled, so that the entire body seemed to twitch and undulate, even while the monster itself did not move. It exhaled. The stink of raw flesh blew down the wilderness.

"Get me out of here," said Eckels. "It was never like this before. I was always sure I'd come through alive. I had good guides, good safaris, and safety. This time, I figured wrong. I've met my match and admit it. This is too much for me to get hold of."

"Don't run," said Lesperance. "Turn around. Hide in the Machine."

"Yes." Eckels seemed to be numb. He looked at his feet as if trying to make them move. He gave a **grunt** of helplessness.

"Eckels!"

He took a few steps, blinking, shuffling.

"Not *that* way!"

The Monster, at the first motion, **lunged** forward with a terrible scream. It covered one hundred yards in six seconds. The rifles jerked up and blazed fire. A windstorm from the beast's mouth engulfed them in the **stench** of slime and old blood. The Monster roared, teeth glittering with sun.

Eckels, not looking back, walked blindly to the edge of the Path, his gun limp in his arms, stepped off the Path, and walked, not knowing it, in the jungle. His feet sank into green **moss**. His legs moved him, and he felt alone and remote from the events behind.

The rifles cracked again. Their sound was lost in shriek and lizard thunder. The great level of the reptile's tail swung up, **lashed** sideways. Trees exploded in clouds of leaf and branch. The Monster twitched its jeweler's hands down to fondle at the men, to twist them in half, to crush them like berries, to cram them into its teeth and its screaming throat. Its boulder-stone eyes levelled with the men. They saw themselves mirrored. They fired at the metallic eyelids and the blazing black iris.

Like a stone idol, like a mountain avalanche, *Tyrannosaurus* fell. Thundering, it clutched trees, pulled them with it. It wrenched and tore the metal path. The men flung themselves back and away. The body hit, ten tons of cold flesh and stone. The guns fired. The Monster lashed its armored tail, twitched its snake jaws, and lay still. A fount of blood **spurted** from its throat. Somewhere inside, a sac of fluids burst. Sickening **gushes drenched** the hunters. They stood, red and glistening.

The thunder faded.

The jungle was silent. After the avalanche, a green peace. After the nightmare, morning.

Billings and Kramer sat on the pathway and threw up[29]. Travis and Lesperance stood with smoking rifles, cursing steadily.

In the Time Machine, on his face, Eckels lay shivering. He had found his way back to the Path, climbed into the Machine.

Travis came walking, glanced at Eckels, took cotton **gauze** from a metal box, and returned to the others, who were sitting on the Path.

"Clean up."

They wiped the blood from their helmets. They began to **curse** too. The Monster lay, a hill of solid flesh. Within, you could hear the sighs and murmurs as the furthest chambers of it died, the organs malfunctioning, liquids running a final instant from pocket to sac to spleen[30], everything shutting off, closing

29 *informal, phrase 'threw up'*: vomit

30 *medical*: the organ in your body that removes dead red cells from your blood and produces white cells

up forever. It was like standing by a wrecked locomotive or a steam shovel at quitting time, all valves being released or levered tight. Bones cracked; the tonnage of its own flesh, off balance, dead weight, **snapped** the delicate forearms, caught underneath. The meat settled, quivering.

Another cracking sound. Overhead, a gigantic tree branch broke from its heavy mooring[31], fell. It crashed upon the dead beast with finality.

"There." Lesperance checked his watch. "Right on time. That's the giant tree that was scheduled to fall and kill this animal originally." He glanced at the two hunters. "You want the trophy picture?"

"What?"

"We can't take a trophy back to the Future. The body has to stay right here where it would have died originally, so the insects, birds, bacteria can get at it, as they were intended to. Everything in balance. The body stays. But we *can* take a picture of you standing near it."

The two men tried to think, but gave up, shaking their heads.

They let themselves be led along the metal Path. They sank wearily into the Machine cushions. They gazed back at the ruined Monster, the **stagnating** mound, where already strange reptilian birds and golden insects were busy at the steaming armor.

A sound on the floor of the Time Machine stiffened them. Eckels sat there, shivering.

"I'm sorry," he said at last.

"Get up!" cried Travis.

Eckels got up.

"Go out on that Path alone," said Travis. He had his rifle pointed. "You're not coming back in the Machine. We're leaving you here!"

Lesperance seized Travis's arm. "Wait –"

"Stay out of this!" Travis shook his hand away. "This fool nearly killed us. But it isn't *that* so much, no. It's his *shoes*! Look

31 where a boat is tied up to the shore

at them! He ran off the Path. That *ruins* us! We'll forfeit[32]! Thousands of dollars of insurance! We guarantee no one leaves the Path. He left it. Oh, the fool! I'll have to report to the government. They might revoke[33] our license[34] to travel. Who knows *what* he's done to Time, to History!"

"Take it easy, all he did was kick up some dirt!"

"How do we *know?*" cried Travis. "We don't know anything! It's all a mystery! Get out of here, Eckels!"

Eckels fumbled his shirt. "I'll pay anything. A hundred thousand dollars!"

Travis glared at Eckels' checkbook and spat. "Go out there. The Monster's next to the Path. Stick your arms up to your elbows in his mouth. Then you can come back with us."

"That's unreasonable!"

"The Monster's dead, you idiot. The bullets! The bullets can't be left behind. They don't belong in the Past; they might change anything. Here's my knife. Dig them out!"

The jungle was alive again, full of the old tremorings[35] and bird cries. Eckels turned slowly to regard the primeval garbage[36] dump, that hill of nightmares and terror. After a long time, like a sleepwalker he shuffled out along the Path.

He returned, shuddering, five minutes later, his arms soaked and red to the elbows. He held out his hands. Each held a number of steel bullets. Then he fell. He lay where he fell, not moving.

"You didn't have to make him do that," said Lesperance.

"Didn't I? It's too early to tell." Travis **nudged** the still body. "He'll live. Next time he won't go hunting game like this. Okay." He jerked his thumb wearily at Lesperance. "Switch on. Let's go home."

1492. 1776[37]. 1812[38].

---

32 be forced to lose a right or benefit because you have broken the law
33 to officially say that something is no longer legal
34 *US spelling:* British spelling is *licence*
35 sounds and movements
36 *US:* British word is *rubbish*
37 the year the United States Declaration of Independence from the British Empire was signed
38 Russia defeated Napoleon, the USA declared war on England

They cleaned their hands and faces. They changed their caking[39] shirts and pants. Eckels was up and around again, not speaking. Travis glared at him for a full ten minutes.

"Don't look at me," cried Eckels. "I haven't done anything."

"Who can tell?"

"Just ran off the Path, that's all, a little mud on my shoes – what do you want me to do – get down and pray?"

"We might need it. I'm warning you, Eckels, I might kill you yet. I've got my gun ready."

"I'm innocent. I've done nothing!"

1999. 2000. 2055.

The Machine stopped.

"Get out," said Travis.

The room was there as they had left it. But not the same as they had left it. The same man sat behind the same desk. But the same man did not quite sit behind the same desk.

Travis looked around swiftly. "Everything okay here?" he snapped.

"Fine. Welcome home!"

Travis did not relax. He seemed to be looking at the very atoms of the air itself, at the way the sun poured through the one high window.

"Okay, Eckels, get out. Don't ever come back."

Eckels could not move.

"You heard me," said Travis. "What're you *staring* at?"

Eckels stood smelling of the air, and there was a thing to the air, a chemical **taint** so subtle, so slight, that only a faint cry of his subliminal senses warned him it was there. The colors, white, gray, blue, orange, in the wall, in the furniture, in the sky beyond the window, were … were … And there was a *feel*. His flesh twitched. His hands twitched. He stood drinking the oddness with the pores of his body. Somewhere, someone must have been screaming one of those whistles that only a dog can hear. His body screamed silence in return. Beyond this room, beyond this wall, beyond this man who was not quite the same man seated at this desk that was not quite the same desk … lay

39 covered in drying blood

an entire world of streets and people. What sort of world it was now, there was no telling. He could feel them moving there, beyond the walls, almost, like so many chess pieces blown in a dry wind …

But the immediate thing was the sign painted on the office wall, the same sign he had read earlier today on first entering.

Somehow, the sign had changed:

> TIME SAFARI INC.
> SAFARIS TU ANY YEER EN THE PAST
> YU NAIM THE ANIMALL.
> WEE TAEKYUTHAIR.
> YU SHOOT ITT.

Eckels felt himself fall into a chair. He fumbled crazily at the thick slime on his boots. He held up a clod of dirt, trembling. "No, it *can't* be. Not a *little* thing like that. No!"

Embedded in the mud, glistening green and gold and black, was a butterfly, very beautiful and very dead.

"Not a little thing like *that*! Not a butterfly!" cried Eckels.

It fell to the floor, an exquisite thing, a small thing that could upset balance and knock down a line of small dominoes and then big dominoes and then gigantic dominoes, all down the years across Time. Eckels' mind whirled. It *couldn't* change things. Killing one butterfly couldn't be *that* important! Could it?

His face was cold. His mouth trembled, asking: "Who – Who won the presidential election yesterday?"

The man behind the desk laughed. "You joking? You know very well. Deutscher, of course! Who else? Not that fool weakling Keith. We got an iron man now, a man with guts!" The official stopped. "What's wrong?"

Eckels **moaned**. He dropped to his knees. He scrabbled at the golden butterfly with shaking fingers. "Can't we," he **pleaded** to the world, to himself, to the officials, to the Machine, "can't we take it *back*, can't we *make* it alive again? Can't we start over? Can't we –"

He did not move. Eyes shut, he waited, shivering. He heard Travis breathe loud in the room; he heard Travis shift his rifle, click the safety catch, and raise the weapon.

There was a sound of thunder.

Post-reading exercises

Understanding the story

1 **Use these questions to help you check that you have understood the story.**

1

1 How does Eckels feel as he reads the sign?
2 What is he worried about?
3 What does he remember as he looks at the time machine?
4 What had happened the day before?
5 What do they think about the new President?
6 What do they think about the candidate who lost?
7 What does the man behind the desk ask Eckels to sign? Why?
8 Why does he invite him to tear his cheque up?

2

9 How many men are there in the time machine?
10 What do we know about them?
11 How many shots does it take to kill a dinosaur?
12 How far back in time have they travelled?
13 What is the Path?
14 Why is it important to stay on the Path?
15 How do they choose which animals to hunt?
16 Why is it impossible for them to know whether the hunt will be a success?
17 How does Eckels feel as they approach the place where they will see the tyrannosaurus?
18 How does he feel when he finally sees it?
19 Why does he refuse to shoot it?
20 Why does he walk off the Path?
21 How do the hunters kill the tyrannosaurus?
22 How did they get covered in blood?
23 Why is everyone cursing?
24 Why don't the hunters want to have their photograph taken?
25 Why does Travis send Eckels out onto the Path again?
26 What is Travis worried will happen when they get back to their time?
27 And what is he worried will already have happened?
28 What changes does Eckels first sense?
29 What is the first material sign of change?

30 What does he take from the mud on the bottom of his boots?
31 How has the world changed?
32 What happens to Eckels at the end?

Language study

One of the main themes of the story is the future consequences of a small, simple action. This is reflected in the language through the use of the modal verbs of speculation: *would, could* and *might.*

Modals of speculation

Form

present or future: **would, could, might** + infinitive (without *to*)
the stomp of your foot on one mouse **could cause** *an earthquake*
past : **would, could, might + have + past participle (been, done)**
from his loins **would have sprung** *ten sons*

Use

We use *would* to explain a logical conclusion of an action or situation.

> *Unless you looked close you* **wouldn't** *see it (but if you looked closely you definitely would).*

> *The body has to stay here where it* **would have died** *originally.*

We use *might* and *could* to discuss possible or alternative consequences, without knowing if they really will (or did) happen.

> *They* **might** *revoke our licence (on the other hand, they might just make us pay a fine).*

We use *couldn't* to say that we think or believe something is impossible.

> *Killing one butterfly* **couldn't be** *that important! Could it?*

These modals of speculation are often used in conditional sentences, with *if* clauses.
1 **If the time travellers hadn't killed the tyrannosaurus,** he would have died anyway.
2 **If time travel ever became possible,** the consequences could get quite complicated.

1 Look at the two *if* clauses above. Which is describing:

a) an imagined situation in the future?
b) an imagined situation in the past?

Notice the verb forms that are used. Choose the correct words to complete this explanation.

An *if* clause with a verb in the *simple past/past perfect* describes an imaginary situation in the past.

An *if* clause with a verb in the *simple past/past perfect* describes an imaginary situation in the future.

2 Look at these examples. Match the verbs in bold to their meanings (a) to (d).

1 *A little error here **would multiply** in sixty million years.*
2 *Queen Elizabeth **might not be born**.*
3 *I'm warning you, Eckels, **I might kill you** yet.*
4 *Crushing certain plants **could add up** infinitesimally.*
5 *We met the Monster not more than two minutes before **he would have died** anyway.*

(a) it's a realistic option
(b) a logical consequence in the past of an imagined past situation
(c) a logical consequence in the future of an imagined situation
(d) one of many possible consequences in the future (x 2)

3 Write the words below in the correct order to form sentences. Start with the words in bold.

1 **If** / the future / stepped / Eckels / wouldn't have / hadn't /changed / off the path

_____

2 **Eckels** / a little more quickly / he'd / escaped / if / might have / reacted

_____

3 **Deutscher** / the butterfly / the election / hadn't / wouldn't have / killed / won / Eckels / if

_____

4 **Keith /** in Eckel's / a better president / would have / opinion / been

_____

5 **The** / from killing / Travis / stopped / Eckels / could have / other hunters

_____

4 Look at the sentences you have just written. Do you agree with them?

5 Imagine what might have happened in the following situations. Write the possible consequences for each situation using modals of speculation.

1 Travis killed Eckels in the past and left him there.
2 The hunters' shots didn't manage to kill the tyrannosaurus.
3 The changes in the future because of the death of the butterfly meant that time travel had not been invented.

Multiple-clause sentences

Bradbury writes with short, concise, simple sentences. He tends to focus on action and words and he only uses complex, multiple-clause sentences on a few occasions. When he does use them it is generally to set the scene.

6 Look at the example below.

The muscles around his mouth formed a smile / as he put his hand slowly out upon the air /, and in that hand waved a check for ten thousand dollars / to the man / behind the desk.

There are five clauses in this sentence. Notice how these clauses can be expanded into simple one-clause sentences.

1 The muscles around his mouth formed a smile.
2 He put his hand slowly out upon the air.
3 In that hand he waved a check for ten thousand dollars.
4 The check was to the man.
5 The man was sitting behind the desk.

7 Compare the original sentence with the five shorter sentences and answer these questions.

1 What words have been cut from the original sentence?
2 What words and phrases have been added to the simpler sentences?
3 What is the difference in effect between the one, long sentence and the series of shorter sentences?
4 What are the advantages of using a complex, multiple-clause sentence when setting the scene?

8 Look at another example. Break it down into six shorter, simpler sentences.

The fog that had enveloped the Machine blew away / and they were in an old time, / a very old time indeed, / three hunters and two Safari Heads /

with their blue metal guns / across their knees.

For more discussion of sentence length and complex clauses see the Style section in *Literary analysis* below.

Literary analysis

Plot

1 What are the main events in the story? Which is the one most important event? Why is it so important?

2 Why did Eckels leave the path? What were the consequences at the time, for the hunt and the hunters?

3 What were the consequences in 2055? What changes had taken place? What were the consequences for Eckels and the Time Safari staff in a society where Deutscher had been elected president? What changes in society does his election represent?

4 Could Eckels' fate at the end of the story have been different? Did he deserve it?

5 What is the story telling us about the consequences of small, insignificant actions?

6 If the death of the butterfly has been responsible for the changes in the future, why are Eckels and the others not affected by these changes as well? (see the notes on 'Time Paradox' in the *Background information* section on page 58). If the story followed the theory more closely, what should have happened when Eckels stood on and killed the butterfly? Does this contradiction affect your enjoyment or appreciation of the story?

Character

7 What do you know about Eckels? What does he feel about the hunt? Why do you think he wanted to go in the first place? Why does he react the way he does? In what way is he different from the other hunters?

8 What do we know about the other hunters? How do they react to the hunt and the killing of the dinosaur?

9 What kind of person is Travis? Choose three adjectives to describe him. Think of examples of his actions and reactions in the story that help explain your choice.

Narration

10   Who is telling the story? Is any one particular view point given? How do we know what the characters are thinking and feeling? Whose thoughts and feelings are described in most detail?

11   There is a lot of dialogue in the story. Find examples where the dialogue is:

a) showing us something about Eckels and his attitude to the hunt

b) explaining the scientific premise of the story

c) explaining the mechanics of the hunt and the time machine.

12   What other functions does the dialogue have?

Style

Similes, metaphors and imagery

Bradbury's style is very rich in similes, metaphors and imagery, particularly when he is trying to put across the wonder of the time machine and the experience of seeing dinosaurs.

Similes and **metaphors** are used to compare a person or thing with another, focusing on similarities and characteristics that they have in common.

Similes are more direct and use the prepositions *like* or *as* to introduce the comparison:

*A sound **like** a giant bonfire burning all of Time*

*Suddenly it all ceased **as** if someone had shut a door*

In the first simile, Bradbury is describing Eckels' first impressions of the time machine. He compares the machine with an enormous fire. In the second simile he is describing how the noise and movements of the prehistoric jungle suddenly stop as the tyrannosaurus approaches. He compares the sudden silence with someone closing a door.

Metaphors are more indirect and often more concise – they describe a person or thing using language that is normally associated with something very different, as when Bradbury describes how it feels to travel back in time:

The Machine howled.

By using the verb *howl*, a verb which describes a noise made by a wild animal, Bradbury is comparing the machine to a wild animal.

13 Look at the description of the time machine. Notice the images
    that are used to describe the machine and its power. Look at the
    words in bold and answer the questions.

    *Eckels glanced across the vast office at a mass and tangle, a **snaking**
    and humming of wires and steel boxes, at an aurora that flickered now
    orange, now silver, now blue. There was a sound **like a gigantic
    bonfire burning all of Time**, all the years and all **the parchment
    calendars**, all the hours **piled high and set aflame**.*

    – What aspect of the machine is being described?
    – What is it being compared to?
    – What is the effect of the comparison?
    – What is the overall effect of the description?

14 Look at the images from the advert for the time machine as Eckels
    remembers it [Page 64]. Explain the images, what associations do
    they have for you?

15 Look at the description of the tyrannosaurus [page 70]. Look at the
    images in bold and answer the questions.

    *It came on great **oiled**, resilient, striding legs. It **towered** thirty
    feet above half of the trees, a great evil god, folding its delicate
    watchmaker's claws close to its oily reptilian chest. Each lower leg
    was a **piston**, a thousand pounds of white bone, sunk in thick **ropes**
    of muscle, sheathed over in a gleam of pebbled skin like **the mail of
    a terrible warrior**. Each thigh was a ton of meat, ivory, and **steel
    mesh**. And from the great breathing cage of the upper body those two
    delicate arms dangled out front, arms with hands which might pick up
    and examine men like toys, while the **snake neck** coiled. And the head
    itself, a ton of **sculptured stone**, lifted easily upon the sky. Its mouth
    gaped, exposing **a fence** of teeth like daggers. Its eyes rolled, **ostrich
    eggs**, empty of all expression save hunger.*

    Which compare the dinosaur to:
    a) a machine
    b) a man
    c) a skyscraper
    d) other creatures

    Which images do you find most effective? Why?

16 Bradbury uses incredible detail and observation in describing the
    tyrannosaurus. Look at the description below and answer the
    questions.

    *The Tyrant Lizard raised itself. Its armoured flesh glittered like a
    thousand green coins. The coins, crusted with **slime**, **steamed**. In the
    slime, **tiny insects wriggled**, so that the entire body seemed **to twitch***

and **undulate**, *even while the monster itself did not move. It exhaled.*
The stink of raw flesh *blew down the wilderness.*
- What senses are these details appealing to?
- Had you ever thought of these details yourself when imagining a dinosaur?
- What is the overall effect of the description?

17 Find other similes and metaphors in the story and analyse their imagery and power. Look in particular at the images used to describe the tyrannosaurus as he falls, the peace and quiet after the tyrannosaurus has been killed or the consequences of killing the butterfly.

18 Look at the last two paragraphs of the story. Look at the simple, repetitive structure of the sentences. What effect is created?

19 Look at the last sentence of the story. Does Bradbury tell us what happens? How do we know what happens? He uses the phrase *a sound of thunder* earlier in the story. What was he referring to? How does this echo add to the power of the last, concluding sentence?

Guidance to the above literary terms, answer keys to all the exercises and activities, plus a wealth of other reading-practice material, can be found on the student's section of the Macmillan Readers website at:
www.macmillanenglish.com/readers.

Travel by Wire!

by Arthur C Clarke

About the author

Arthur C Clarke was a famous British science-fiction writer. His best-known work is the novel *2001: Space Odyssey*, which he wrote with the film producer Stanley Kubrick. He had a lifelong interest in science and especially in astronomy. In addition to his science-fiction works, he also wrote books about space and space travel and was awarded the Kalinga Prize[1] in 1961 for the popularisation of science. In 1994, he was nominated for the Nobel Peace Prize and in 1999, for the Nobel Prize in literature.

Clarke was born in Minehead, Somerset, in December 1917. As a boy he was interested in both astronomy and science-fiction stories. He left school at 18 and moved to London, where he joined the British Interplanetary Society and started writing science fiction.

When the Second World War started, he joined the Royal Air Force as a radar specialist. He worked on a new radar system, which would come into operation at the end of the war, and he was promoted to chief training instructor at a specialist RAF training centre. At the end of the war he entered King's College London to study maths and physics.

Clarke was one of the first people to write about the concept of geostationary satellites[2] and their possible uses in communication technology, 25 years before they actually came into use. The geostationary orbit 36,000 feet above the equator is named the Clarke Orbit in his honour.

Clarke first started writing science-fiction stories in fanzines[3] between 1937 and 1945. His first professional story, *Rescue Party* was published in *Astounding Science Fiction* in 1946. He started writing full time in 1951. In his long writing career, which continued until his death in 2008 at the age of 90, he wrote more than 34 novels and more than 20 short-story collections as well as numerous non-fiction books.

1 an award given by UNESCO for exceptional skills in presenting scientific ideas to people with no scientific background
2 a satellite in orbit around the Earth which seems not to move because it travels at the same speed as the Earth
3 non-professional science-fiction magazines

He won all three of the most prestigious science-fiction awards, the Nebula, the Hugo and the John Campbell awards, and in 1986, he was named a Grand Master by the Science Fiction Writers of America. In 2000, he was given a knighthood by the Queen and became Sir Arthur C Clarke.

About the story

Travel By Wire! is Arthur C Clarke's first published story. It was first published in December 1937 in the magazine *Amateur Science Stories*. It was subsequently published as part of *The Best of Arthur C. Clarke 1937–1955*, a short-story collection.

The story is set in the UK in the 1960s. A group of scientists have developed a means of *teleporting*, that is of instantly transporting people from one place to another.

Background information

Teleportation

The ability to instantly transfer objects from one place to another may not be as impossible as we think. Research in recent years has shown that the teleportation of individual atoms is possible through a technique called 'quantum entanglement'. Some physicists suggest that by the end of the century we will have found a way to teleport larger objects, and possibly also human beings.

Scanners

Early scanners were first developed in the 1920s. They were used to send copies of documents or photographs using telephone lines. These scanners were also used in early TV technology. The scanners described in the story – 3D scanners which are capable of copying the dimensions of an object and recreating it on a computer screen – were not developed until almost 60 years after the story was written.

TV

The first TVs were developed in the late 1920s and early 1930s. Clarke shows an awareness of this technology and an understanding of the science involved. His radio-transporter, is, in part, based on the scientific ideas behind the development of early TVs.

Summary

It may help you to know something about what happens in the story before you read it. Don't worry, this summary does *not* tell you how the story ends!

The story tells the history of the discovery and development of a radio-transporter; a machine that can send people from one destination to another instantly, by means of a cable.

The first object to be transported was a block of wood. The experiment was a partial success, and after some further improvements, the inventors succeeded in transporting a guinea pig. There was, however, one problem: the guinea pig was dead. After further studies and improvements, they succeeded, not only in transporting a living guinea pig, but also in transporting a person.

Once the inventors had also succeeded in transporting themselves through the machine, they were ready to show their invention in public. Soon they were ready to start a commercial transporting service. The first service took place between London and Paris and the radio-transporter soon became a great success. Services were provided between all the big cities in Europe, and the larger towns in each country.

The system was not perfect, and accidents did sometimes happen. But as an unexpected result of one particular problem, the inventors discovered that their machine could help people lose weight, and so a new application for the machine was developed.

The story closes with a slightly worrying statement from one of the inventors.

Pre-reading exercises

Key vocabulary

This section will help you familiarise yourself with some of the more specific vocabulary used in the story. You may want to use it to help you before you start reading, or as a revision exercise after you have finished the story.

Scientific terminology

In describing the radio-transporter, the inventor uses some technical terms.

1 **Look at the terms in bold below and their definitions. What technology do you associate each word with?**

a) TV
b) medicine
c) physics
d) computers

Appleton Q layer a band of ionised gases in the Earth's atmosphere. It acts as a reflector of radio signals

chloroform a clear liquid with a strong smell that makes you unconscious if you breathe it. It was used in the past in medical operations.

definition the clear edges or shape that something has that makes it easy to see

delta ray a term often used in science fiction to describe a fictional type of ray or radiation

fuse a part of a piece of electrical equipment that makes it stop working when there is too much electricity flowing through it; *blow a fuse* to make the fuse operate and stop the equipment from working

induction the production of electrical or magnetic forces in an object by other electrical or magnetic forces near it

interference radio signals that make the sound or picture of a radio or TV programme difficult to hear or see clearly

polyaxial cable if something is **polyaxial** it is very flexible and allows movement in a number of different directions

resistance coils normally referred to as **resistors**: a piece of wire or other material that controls the level of electrical current flowing in a circuit by providing resistance (the ability to stop the flow of electricity)

respirator an object covering your nose and mouth that helps you to breathe when you are in a place that is full of smoke or gas

---

2 **Find these terms in the extracts below. Do they refer to:**

a) real, existing scientific phenomena and technology?
b) technology invented by the author for the purposes of this story?

1 *The greatest difficulty, as it had been in television thirty years before, was improving definition, and we spent nearly five years over that little problem.*

2 *This we managed to do by using the delta-ray scanners all round our subject, above, below, right, left, in front and behind.*

3 *We obtained another guinea pig, chloroformed it, and sent it through the transmitter.*

4 We had to work in respirators for a month.
5 We drew the line, though, at Lord Rosscastle, who would have blown the fuses even if we could have got him into the transmitter.
6 We also had a good deal of trouble through interference and induction. You see, our apparatus picked up various electrical disturbances and superimposed them on the object under transmission.
7 We made a special apparatus which transmitted massive dowagers (rich, elderly women) round resistance coils and reassembled them where they started.
8 A wired system was safer, though it was dreadfully difficult to lay polyaxial cables, costing £500 a mile, under the Channel.
9 Even the micro-waves are stopped by the Appleton 'Q' layer at 100,000 km, you know.

Idiomatic expressions

The speaker in the story mixes formal, scientific language with informal, spoken language containing idiomatic expressions.

3 **Look at the idiomatic expressions in bold in the extracts below. Match them to the definitions and explanations (a) to (f).**

1 That is the best of being **in our line**, you can always do what you like with the other people.
2 The chemists on the next floor were our only serious rivals, but we generally **came out on top**.
3 One evening old Professor Hudson stayed behind and we nearly **finished him off**.
4 We **drew the line**, though, at Lord Rosscastle, who would have blown the fuses even if we could have got him into the transmitter.
5 Perhaps one day we'd **heap coals of fire on their heads** by sending them a few millions.
6 Many people came out looking **like nothing on earth** and very little on Mars or Venus.

(a) to be the best or the winner
(b) to say that you will definitely not allow or accept something
(c) to kill someone, can be used literally or as an exaggeration
(d) a saying that comes from the Bible: it means to punish your enemies by being kind to them, (so that they feel that they are in debt to you)

(e) working in a certain profession or job

(f) very good or very bad

4 In which idiom is the writer using both the idiomatic and the literal meaning of the expression?

5 Use the expressions above to complete these sentences.

1 I had eaten an enormous meal and was feeling really full, so the ice cream at the end almost .... me .... !

2 I was happy to clean the floors and make the food but I .... at looking after the dogs.

3 No matter who he's competing against, he always ....

4 Being firefighters, danger and adventure are day to day realities ....

5 Her chocolate cakes were wonderful, they were ....

6 If your enemy is hungry, feed him; if he is thirsty, give him to drink; for in so doing you will ....'

Main themes

Before you read the story, you may want to think about some of the main themes that come up. The questions will help you think about the story as you are reading it for the first time. There is more discussion of the main themes in the *Literary analysis* section after the story.

Discoveries and inventions

The main theme of the story is the relationship between inventors and their discoveries. Some inventions are made for the good of man, some are made in order to make a lot of money. Some inventors are modest and are not interested in appearing in public, others enjoy the fame that results from their inventions.

6 As you read the story, decide if the inventor in the story is mainly interested in:

a) the general good of humanity and the progress of science

b) becoming famous

c) making a lot of money.

7 As you read the story, think of the invention and answer these questions:

a) what is the initial purpose of the invention?
b) what other money-making use do they find for it?
c) what use are they thinking of for the future?

Commercialisation

The story is a gentle satire (a piece of literature that uses humour to criticise someone or something) of the world of business and innovation. It looks at how the basic scientific principle is exploited, and how the idea is sold to the general public, as well as how the public responds to it.

8 As you read the story, think about:

a) how the machine is first introduced to the public
b) how the public responds to it and the accidents that happen.

Think about an innovative new product that has been marketed recently. Are there any similarities in the way it was developed and marketed?

Travel by Wire!

by Arthur C Clarke

You people can have no idea of the troubles and trials we had to **endure** before we perfected the radio-transporter, not that it's quite perfect even yet. The greatest difficulty, as it had been in television thirty years before, was improving definition, and we spent nearly five years over that little problem. As you will have seen in the Science Museum, the first object we transmitted was a wooden cube, which was assembled all right, only instead of being one solid block it consisted of millions of little spheres. In fact, it looked just like a solid edition of one of the early television pictures, for instead of dealing with the object molecule by molecule or better still electron by electron, our scanners took little chunks at a time.

This didn't matter for some things, but if we wanted to transmit objects of art, let alone human beings, we would have to improve the process considerably. This we managed to do by using the delta-ray scanners all round our subject, above, below, right, left, in front and behind. It was a lovely game **synchronizing** all six, I can tell you, but when it was done we found that the transmitted elements were ultra-microscopic in size, which was quite good enough for most purposes.

Then, when they weren't looking, we borrowed a guinea pig from the biology people on the 37th floor, and sent it through the apparatus. It came through in excellent condition, except for the fact it was dead. So we had to return it to its owner with a polite request for a **post-mortem**. They raved a bit at first, saying that the unfortunate creature had been **inoculated** with the only specimens of some germs they'd spent months **rearing** from the bottle. They were so annoyed, in fact, that they flatly refused our request.

Such **insubordination** on the part of mere biologists was of course **deplorable**, and we promptly generated a high-frequency field in their laboratory and gave them all fever for a few minutes. The post-mortem results came up in half an hour, the verdict being that the creature was in perfect condition but had died of shock, with a **rider** to the effect that if we wanted to try the experiment again we should blindfold our victims. We were also told that a combination lock had been fitted to the 37th floor to protect it from the depredations[4] of kleptomaniacal[5] mechanics who should be washing cars in a garage. We could not let this pass, so we immediately X-rayed their lock and to their complete **consternation** told them what the key-word was.

That is the best of being in our line, you can always do what you like with the other people. The chemists on the next floor were our only serious rivals, but we generally came out on top. Yes, I remember that time they slipped some **vile** organic stuff into our lab through a hole in the ceiling. We had to work in respirators for a month, but we had our revenge later. Every night after the staff had left, we used to send a dose of mild cosmics into the lab and **curdled** all their beautiful precipitates, until one evening old Professor Hudson stayed behind and we nearly finished him off. But to get back to my story –

We obtained another guinea pig, chloroformed it, and sent it through the transmitter. To our delight, it revived. We immediately had it killed and **stuffed** for the benefit of posterity. You can see it in the museum with the rest of our apparatus.

But if we wanted to start a passenger service, this would never do – it would be too much like an operation to suit most people. However, by cutting down the transmitting time to a ten-thousandth of a second, and thus reducing the shock, we managed to send another guinea pig in full possession of its faculties. This one is also stuffed.

The time had obviously come for one of us to try out the apparatus but as we realised what a loss it would be to humanity should anything go wrong, we found a suitable victim in the person of Professor Kingston, who teaches Greek or something

4 *formal*: damage or harm that is done to something
5 addicted to stealing things

foolish on the 197th floor. We **lured** him to the transmitter with a copy of *Homer*, switched on the field, and by the **row** from the receiver, we knew he'd arrived safely and in full possession of his faculties, such as they were. We would have liked to have had him stuffed as well, but it couldn't be arranged.

After that we went through in turns, found the experience quite painless, and decided to put the device on the market. I expect you can remember the excitement there was when we first demonstrated our little toy to the Press. Of course we had the dickens[6] of a job convincing them that it wasn't a fake, and they didn't really believe it until they had been through the transporter themselves. We drew the line, though, at Lord Rosscastle, who would have blown the fuses even if we could have got him into the transmitter.

This demonstration gave us so much publicity that we had no trouble at all in forming a company. We bade a reluctant farewell to the Research Foundation, told the remaining scientists that perhaps one day we'd heap coals of fire on their heads by sending them a few millions, and started to design our first commercial senders and receivers.

The first service was inaugurated on May 10th, 1962. The ceremony took place in London, at the transmitting end, though at the Paris receiver there were enormous crowds watching to see the first passengers arrive, and probably hoping they wouldn't. Amid cheers from the assembled thousands, the Prime Minister pressed a button (which wasn't connected to anything), the chief engineer threw a switch (which was) and a large Union Jack[7] faded from view and appeared again in Paris, rather to the annoyance of some patriotic Frenchmen.

After that, passengers began to stream through at a rate which left the Customs officials helpless. The service was a great and instantaneous success, as we only charged £2[8] per person. This we considered very moderate, for the electricity used cost quite one-hundredth of a penny.

6 *old-fashioned*: used to suggest that something is difficult and complicated
7 the national flag of the UK
8 approximately £75 today

Before long we had services to all the big cities of Europe, by cable that is, not radio. A wired system was safer, though it was dreadfully difficult to lay polyaxial cables, costing £500 a mile, under the Channel[9]. Then, in conjunction with the Post Office, we began to develop internal services between the large towns. You may remember our slogans 'Travel by Phone' and 'It's quicker by Wire' which were heard everywhere in 1963. Soon, practically everyone used our circuits and we were handling thousands of tons of **freight** per day.

Naturally, there were accidents, but we could point out that we had done what no Minister of Transport had ever done, reduced road fatalities to a mere ten thousand a year. We lost one client in six million, which was pretty good even to start with, though our record is even better now. Some of the **mishaps** that occurred were very peculiar indeed, and in fact there are quite a few cases which we haven't explained to the **dependents**[10] yet, or to the insurance companies either.

One common complaint was earthing along the line. When that happened, our unfortunate passenger was just dissipated into nothingness. I suppose his or her molecules would be distributed more or less evenly over the entire earth. I remember one particularly **gruesome** accident when the apparatus failed in the middle of a transmission. You can guess the result … Perhaps even worse was what happened when two lines got crossed and the currents were mixed.

Of course, not all accidents were as bad as these. Sometimes, owing to a high resistance in the circuit, a passenger would lose anything up to five stone[11] in transit, which generally cost us about £1000 and enough free meals to restore the missing embonpoint[12]. Fortunately, we were soon able to make money out of this affair, for fat people came along to be reduced to manageable dimensions. We made a special apparatus which transmitted massive dowagers[13] round resistance coils and

9 the English Channel: the strip of water separating England and France
10 US spelling: British spelling is dependant
11 approximately 32 kg
12 old-fashioned: fat
13 a woman who has a title or property because her husband belonged to a high social class, used informally to refer to an impressive older lady, especially one who is rich

reassembled them where they started, minus the cause of the trouble. 'So quick, my dear, and *quite* painless! I'm *sure* they could take off that 150 pounds[14] you want to lose in no time! Or is it 200[15]?'

We also had a good deal of trouble through interference and induction. You see, our apparatus picked up various electrical disturbances and superimposed them on the object under transmission. As a result many people came out looking like nothing on earth and very little on Mars or Venus. They could usually be straightened out by the plastic surgeons, but some of the products had to be seen to be believed.

Fortunately these difficulties have been largely overcome now that we use the micro-beams for our carrier, though now and then accidents still occur. I expect you remember that big lawsuit we had last year with Lita Cordova, the television star, who claimed £1,000,000 damages from us for alleged loss of beauty. She asserted that one of her eyes had moved during a transmission, but I couldn't see any difference myself and nor could the jury, who had enough opportunity. She had hysterics in the court when our Chief Electrician went into the box and said bluntly, to the alarm of both side's lawyers, that if anything really *had* gone wrong with the transmission, Miss Cordova wouldn't have been able to recognize herself had any cruel person handed her a mirror.

Lots of people ask us when we'll have a service to Venus or Mars. Doubtless that will come in time, but of course the difficulties are pretty considerable. There is so much sun static in space, not to mention the various reflecting layers everywhere. Even the micro-waves are stopped by the Appleton 'Q' layer at 100,000 km, you know. Until we can pierce that, Interplanetary shares are still safe.

Well, I see it's nearly 22, so I'd best be leaving. I have to be in New York by midnight. What's that? Oh no, I'm going by plane. *I* don't travel by wire! You see, I helped invent the thing.

Rockets for me! Good night!

14 approximately 68 kg
15 approximately 90 kg

Post-reading exercises

Understanding the story

1 Use these questions to help you check that you have understood the story.

1 Who is speaking?
2 Who is he or she speaking to?
3 What was the biggest problem they faced?
4 What does the wooden cube in the Science Museum look like?
5 How did they improve the process?
6 Where did they get the guinea pig from?
7 What was it being used for at the time?
8 What happened to the guinea pig?
9 How did they persuade the biology department to perform a post-mortem?
10 What was the conclusion of the post-mortem?
11 What advice did they offer the inventors?
12 What is the inventor's attitude to the other scientists working at the same institution?
13 What happened to the second guinea pig?
14 Where are the second and third guinea pigs now?
15 Who was the first person to try the machine?
16 Why didn't the inventors want to try it themselves at first?
17 How did they persuade the journalists that the machine wasn't a fake?
18 What was the first object to be transported publicly?
19 Where did it travel from?
20 Where did it arrive?
21 Was the service a success?
22 Where did people go to travel from town to town?
23 Was their safety record better or worse than travelling by car?
24 What kind of problems did they have?
25 Which problem gave them a new money-making idea?
26 What did the TV star complain about?
27 Why didn't she win her court case?
28 Why is space travel not a realistic proposition?
29 How is the speaker going to travel to New York?
30 Why doesn't he travel by wire?

Language study

Linkers

Linkers like *however*, *because*, *therefore* connect phrases, clauses and sentences. They show how the ideas in a text connect with each other. They can express a number of different relationships, eg addition, contrast, cause and effect.

1 Look at the use of *though* in the sentence below.

We lost one client in six million, which was pretty good even to start with, ***though*** *our record is even better now.*

Though is used to **contrast** the radio-transporter's record safety in the early days with its record at the time of speaking.

2 Look at the linkers in the extracts below. Match them to their uses.

The first object we transmitted was a wooden cube, which was assembled all right, only (1) ***instead of*** *being one solid block it consisted of millions of little spheres. (2)* ***In fact****, it looked just like a solid edition of one of the early television pictures.*

This didn't matter for some things, but if we wanted to transmit objects of art, (3) ***let alone*** *human beings, we would have to improve the process considerably.*

It came through in excellent condition, (4) ***except for*** *the fact it was dead.*

You see, our apparatus picked up various electrical disturbances and superimposed them on the object under transmission.

(5) ***However****, by cutting down the transmitting time to a ten-thousandth of a second ... we managed to send another guinea pig in full possession of its faculties.*

(6) ***As a result*** *many people came out looking like nothing on earth and very little on Mars or Venus.*

There is so much sun static in space, (7) ***not to mention*** *the various reflecting layers everywhere.*

a) used to introduce the only thing, person or fact that is not included
b) used to add an important extra piece of information
c) used for saying that something is even more difficult than another difficult thing
d) used to explain the consequences of an action or situation
e) used for contrasting with a previous statement

f) used to say that one person, thing or action replaces another

g) used to say what is really true

3 Match the clauses and sentences a–g with the clauses or sentences in 1–7. Underline the linkers.

a) The process was far from perfect at the beginning.

b) The machine was very popular and started making a lot of money.

c) They didn't think they'd be able to transport living organisms,

d) They became rich and famous,

e) They spent their money on expensive clothes, cars and holidays,

f) Everyone was very happy for them, and wished them the best of luck,

g) They decided to use cable to transport people

1 except for their rivals in the biology department.

2 However, they soon managed to solve most of the problems.

3 As a result the inventors were able to leave their jobs at the university.

4 not to mention the various houses, flats and villas they bought.

5 instead of radio waves, because it was safer.

6 in fact, so famous they had to travel with bodyguards.

7 let alone animals or human beings.

4 Complete the sentences below using the linkers in the box.

| as a result   except for   however   in fact   instead of   let alone |
| not to mention |

1 I really enjoyed my holiday, ... the last day when it rained all day.

2 I hardly have time to think these days, ... relax.

3 He was a perfect host, really friendly and hospitable, ... his wonderful cooking.

4 I had to spend all day working .... going to the beach as I had planned!

5 She worked really hard for her exams, and .... she got straight As.

6 We enjoyed the film. .... , I wouldn't really recommend it for children.

7 It was a great film. .... , I think it should win the Oscar.

Multiple-clause sentences

As part of his story-telling style, the inventor sometimes uses long, multiple-clause sentences to add humorous comments to the description of events and situations.

5 Look at the extracts below. Notice how the writer has separated the clauses.

Amid cheers from the assembled thousands, the Prime Minister pressed a button (which wasn't connected to anything), the chief engineer threw a switch (which was) and a large Union Jack faded from view and appeared again in Paris, rather to the annoyance of some patriotic Frenchmen.

6 There are eight clauses in the sentence. Rewrite them as eight separate sentences.

1 There were cheers …

2 The Prime Minister …

3 The button …

4 The chief engineer …

5 The switch …

6 A large Union Jack …

7 It appeared …

8 This annoyed …

7 Look at another extract. How many clauses are there in this sentence?

We lured him to the transmitter with a copy of Homer, *switched on the field, and by the row from the receiver, we knew he'd arrived safely and in full possession of his faculties, such as they were.*

Literary analysis

Plot

1 The plot is fairly simple. It outlines the steps involved in producing and commercialising the radio-transporter. What are the main events described in the story?
2 Which events are a) key events in the process, and b) events that add colour or interest? Write a one-sentence summary of the story.
3 What do you think will happen next?
4 What is the message of the story? What is it telling us about commercialisation? Has the message dated or is it still true today?

Character

5 There is only one main character. What do we know about this character? Is he/she a man or a woman? How old is he/she? What nationality is he/she? Choose three adjectives to describe him/her.
6 The speaker's attitude to the machine is sometimes childish, and sometimes arrogant. Find examples of actions and comments that show these two characteristics.
7 The speaker uses *we* and *us* throughout the story. Who are the other people being referred to? How many people were involved in the invention?

Narration

8 Where is the story being told? Who is it being told to? Why is it being told? What effect does this have on the way the story is told?
9 Is the narrator reliable (can the narrator be trusted)? Can we believe everything the narrator tells us? Is the narrator's point of view objective?

Style

10 The story is told as a monologue and the speaker often refers to the listeners, including them in the story with asides (comments made to the listeners which is not part of the main story) such as:

As you will have seen in the Science Museum …

I expect you can remember the excitement there was when we first demonstrated our little toy to the Press.

You may remember our slogans 'Travel by Phone' and 'It's quicker by Wire'…

What is the effect of these asides?

Can you find other examples where the speaker addresses the audience directly? How does the relationship with the listeners help bring the author's imaginary world to life?

11 The speaker often uses understatement (describing things as being smaller or less important than they really are). Look at these examples:

*The greatest difficulty, as it had been in television thirty years before, was improving definition, and we spent nearly five years over **that little problem**.*

*This we managed to do by using the delta-ray scanners all round our subject, above, below, right, left, in front and behind. It was **a lovely game** synchronizing all six, I can tell you.*

*We **borrowed** a guinea pig from the biology people on the 37th floor.*

What is the effect of these understatements? What do they tell us about the speaker's attitude to the discovery? What is the writer telling us about inventors in general?

12 The speaker often makes short, humorous comments, such as the ones below:

*It came through in excellent condition, **except for the fact it was dead**.*

*We found a suitable victim in the person of Professor Kingston, who teaches Greek **or something foolish** on the 197th floor.*

*At the Paris receiver there were enormous crowds watching to see the first passengers arrive, and **probably hoping they wouldn't**.*

*a large Union Jack faded from view and appeared again in Paris, **rather to the annoyance of some patriotic Frenchmen**.*

What exactly is the joke being made each time? What is the effect of these comments? Do you find them funny? Why/why not?

13 One comment is echoed three times:

*We obtained another guinea pig, chloroformed it, and sent it through the transmitter. To our delight, it revived. We immediately had it killed and **stuffed for the benefit of posterity**. You can see it in the museum with the rest of our apparatus.*

*However, by cutting down the transmitting time to a ten-thousandth of a second, and thus reducing the shock, we managed to send another guinea pig in full possession of its faculties. **This one is also stuffed**.*

*We would have liked to have had him **stuffed** as well, but it couldn't be arranged.*

What is the effect of the repetition? What does it tell us about the inventors and their attitude to their invention?

14   Look at the words used to refer to the passengers in the following extracts:

*Soon, practically everyone used our circuits and we were handling **thousands of tons of freight** per day.*

*We lost **one client** in six million, which was pretty good even to start with, though our record is even better now.*

*As a result many people came out looking like nothing on earth and very little on Mars or Venus. They could usually be straightened out by the plastic surgeons, but some of **the products** had to be seen to be believed.*

What are the people being described as? What does this tell us about the inventor's attitude to the people who use their invention?

15   Look at the closing paragraphs. What is the effect of the last two paragraphs? What is the speaker saying with the words *I don't travel by wire*? What is the writer saying about scientific discoveries in general?

Guidance to the above literary terms, answer keys to all the exercises and activities, plus a wealth of other reading-practice material, can be found on the student's section of the Macmillan Readers website at: www.macmillanenglish.com/readers.

The Martian Odyssey

by Stanley G Weinbaum

About the author

Stanley Graham Weinbaum was a US short-story writer and novelist. His writing career was tragically short. He died of cancer only 18 months after publishing his first, and most influential, science-fiction story: *The Martian Odyssey*.

Weinbaum was born in Kentucky. He attended the University of Wisconsin, studying first chemical engineering and then English literature. He did not finish his degree, and left university in 1923.

Although he was a very important writer, very little is known today about his life. Even his birth date is unknown. Some biographers claim he was born in 1900, while others say 1902. However, everyone agrees that he was born in Kentucky, studied in Wisconsin and lived and worked in Milwaukee.

His first written work, a romance novel entitled *The Lady Dances*, was published in 1934. In his very short writing career he produced a phenomenal body of work. During the 18 months between the publication of his first science-fiction short story, *The Martian Odyssey*, and his death in December 1935, he wrote and published 17 science-fiction stories. Another 11 stories were published after his death.

Weinbaum is held to be one of the most important of the early science-fiction writers in the US, and one who brought a new style and focus to the genre.

About the story

The Martian Odyssey was published in July 1934 in the science-fiction magazine *Wonder Stories*. It was the first of Weinbaum's science-fiction stories and has become his best-known work. It is also the first of two stories that tell of the adventures of Jarvis and his co-astronauts on Mars.

It was a ground-breaking story in its time and immediately established Weinbaum as a leading science-fiction writer. It has been claimed that its influence was so great, it changed the way all subsequent science-fiction stories were written. It was the first story to create an alien character who was sympathetic and intelligent, but very different from man.

The Martian Odyssey is the oldest story to be included in the Science Fiction Writers of America's list of the best science-fiction stories of all time. It came second to Isaac Asimov's *Nightfall*.

Background information

Mars

Mars is the fourth planet from the sun in the solar system. It is visible from Earth with the naked eye and is sometime called the Red Planet because of its reddish appearance. Mars has a thin atmosphere, and its surface is similar to that of the moon, with its craters[1]. It is also in some ways similar to Earth with volcanoes, valleys, deserts and polar ice caps. Its seasonal cycles are also similar to Earth. It has two small, irregularly shaped moons, Phobos and Deimos.

The first maps of Mars were drawn in 1840, but the main geographical features were not named until 1877, when an Italian astronomer, Giovanni Schiaparelli, used a 22 cm telescope to produce the first detailed map of Mars. It was believed at the time that there was water on the surface of Mars; seas, oceans and rivers. Schiaparelli gave them Latin names, many of which remain today (Mare Chronium, Mare Cimmerium). It was not until the 1960s that astronomers found that there was no surface water on Mars, and therefore no potential for life.

Weinbaum's story shows a very detailed knowledge of the astronomy of Mars as it was when the story was written. All the place names he refers to are real. He knew of Mars' thin atmosphere and lack of water, as well as theories about its chemical make up. His description of Mars and his imagined Martian creatures are all true to the information available about Mars in the 1930s.

---

1 a large round hole on the surface of a planet caused by a meteorite hitting it

Summary

It may help you to know something about what happens in the story before you read it. Don't worry, this summary does *not* tell you how the story ends!

A crew of four astronauts are the first men to set foot on Mars. Jarvis, one of the crew, has just been rescued by his fellow astronauts and brought back to their rocket, the *Ares*. He tells the tale of his adventures.

Ten days earlier he had set off in his rocket to film the landscape on Mars. He had just decided to head back to the main rocket when his engines failed and he crashed to the ground. Instead of waiting with his rocket in the hope that the rest of the crew would find him he decided to try to walk back to the *Ares*.

He walked on for as long as he had daylight and then chose a place to stop for the night. He was about to climb into his sleeping bag when he heard a strange noise. He went to explore the cause of the noise and saw two strange creatures fighting each other. One was a black creature with tentacles and it appeared to be attacking a large bird. At first Jarvis did not want to interfere, but then he noticed that the bird-like creature was wearing a bag around its neck. He took this as a sign that the creature was intelligent and so decided to help it.

The bird-like creature put its hands out to Jarvis in a sign of thanks and the two made friends. Jarvis looked around for material to build a fire and the Martian helped him. They both sat down in front of the fire and Jarvis tried to communicate with his new Martian friend, Tweel. They managed to exchange a few words and gestures, but no real communication was possible. In the end Jarvis climbed into his sleeping bag and went to sleep.

When he woke up the next day, Tweel was still there and when he set off on his long walk back to the rocket, Tweel came with him. They walked for two days. On the third day they came across a line of small pyramids stretching across the desert. Jarvis calculated that the oldest might be as much as 500,000 years old. As they walked along, the pyramids got larger and newer until they reached the last one, which was still occupied. They watched as a strange silver creature climbed out of the pyramid, and then immediately started building another, with bricks that it produced from its mouth. Jarvis examined the creature and discovered that it was made of silicon.

They continued on their way and Jarvis, feeling tired and homesick, started to think about a girl he knew back home. Suddenly the girl was there in front of him in the middle of the Martian desert. Jarvis ran towards her, but Tweel stopped him and shot at the girl with his steam gun. The image of the girl disappeared. In its place stood a tentacled creature like the one that had been attacking Tweel when Jarvis first saw him. Tweel's shot had killed the monster. Tweel had saved Jarvis's life.

Again they continued on their way until they reached a canal and a mud city in the distance. As they walked towards the city, they caught sight of first one, and then a row of strange, barrel-shaped creatures. They were pushing small carts and were rushing around carrying stones and sand down into an underground tunnel. Jarvis decided to investigate and Tweel followed him. Soon they were lost. They wandered around for hours, or possibly even days. Eventually they came across a room, and in the room there was a strange machine. The barrel-shaped creatures pushed their carts up to the machine and emptied the contents under its wheels to be crushed to powder. Some of the creatures abandoned their carts and allowed themselves to be crushed too.

Behind the machine stood a small crystal. Jarvis went up to it. As he approached the crystal it shone its light on him and a wart on his thumb dried up and fell off. The crystal seemed to have some sort of healing power. Jarvis thought it would make a great present to take back to Earth. At that moment, however, the cart pushing creatures attacked Jarvis and Tweel. Tweel distracted the creatures by starting a fire, and they managed to escape from the tunnel. But the creatures followed them and started shooting at them. It looked like their end was near when an army of barrel-creatures suddenly appeared from the tunnel.

Pre-reading exercises

Key vocabulary

This section will help you familiarise yourself with some of the more specific vocabulary used in the story. You may want to use it to help you before you start reading, or as a revision exercise after you have finished the story.

Describing the creatures that live on Mars

Jarvis meets a number of strange creatures on his trek across Mars. He describes them all in detail, comparing them to animals and plants on Earth.

Body parts

1 **Look at the words in bold below and their definitions. Match them to the animals and plants in the box.**

> a crab   an eagle   an elephant   a fish   a flower   grass   an octopus

beak the hard curved or pointed part of a bird's mouth
blade a long thin leaf
claw the sharp curved end of the leg of a sea creature that it uses for catching things
scale one of the small, hard, flat pieces of skin on the body of a snake or other similar animal
stem the long thin central part of a plant
talon one of the sharp nails on the feet of a bird that kills other animals for food
tentacle a long, thin arm that is used for moving or for holding things
trunk a long, thin, flexible nose

Movements

2 **Look at the verbs in bold in the sentences below. Match them to their definitions (a) to (i).**

1 Ants were **crawling** all over the food.
2 I **dashed** out into the street, still in my pyjamas.
3 The cat escaped from the dog by **leaping** up a tree.
4 An angler fish **lures** smaller fish into its mouth by means of a light at the end of its tail.
5 The lion **prowled** quietly through the long grass.

6 They were all **scurrying** around like mice.

7 Whenever I go shopping, my dog just **tags along** too.

8 The grey horse came **trotting** across the field.

9 He **trudged** through deep snow to the village.

(a) to go somewhere with someone else even though you're not needed

(b) to move using four or more legs, often used for small insects

(c) to move quietly and slowly, in search of something to eat or hunt

(d) to attract their prey (the animals they want to eat)

(e) to walk somewhere with slow, heavy steps

(f) to leave or go somewhere very quickly because you are in a hurry

(g) to move more quickly than a walk, but without running

(h) to jump into the air or over a long distance

(i) to move fast with quick little steps

3 Use the verbs to complete the sentences below.

a) I'd heard that there were thieves .... around the area at night.

b) They .... through the narrow tunnel on their hands and feet.

c) The small dog .... alongside its master.

d) The local hotels are trying to .... tourists back to the area.

e) People were forced to .... to safety from the burning building.

f) I asked if I could .... and he said yes, so long as I kept my mouth shut.

g) He .... slowly home, with his head down and his hands in his pockets.

h) He .... to the window to see what was happening, but he was too late.

i) I heard the sound of little footsteps that were .... along under the roof.

Sounds

4 Look at the verbs and their definitions. Use them to complete the sentences below.

---

boom to make a deep, loud sound that continues for a long time
cackle to laugh in a loud, unpleasant and sometimes unkind way
caw to make a loud, unpleasant noise like a crow (a large black bird)
cluck to make a sound like a chicken
creak a high, sharp sound like that of a door opening
drum to make a continuous sound by hitting a hard surface
rustle to make a sound like sheets of paper or leaves make when they move
screech or squeal to make a loud, high and unpleasant noise like a car braking suddenly
trill a musical sound made by playing or singing two similar notes one after the other very quickly
twitter to make a high, soft, singing sound; used for birds

---

1 The step .... under his foot as he went up to bed trying not to wake his parents.
2 She heard someone .... loudly at the door and ran to see what was happening.
3 The wind .... the leaves in the trees outside her window.
4 She .... in an evil way, just like some old witch.
5 The sound of .... came from the farm as the farmer collected the eggs.
6 A bird .... a beautiful song.
7 At dawn you could hear hundreds of birds .... in the garden.
8 It was raining very heavily, and in the distance thunder ....
9 They heard tyres .... and then a horrible crashing sound as the two cars collided.
10 The crows in the old tower .... loudly and flew up into the air.

Transcribing Putz and Leroy's English

Putz and Leroy are German and French. Their English is good, but not perfect. Putz in particular has a fairly strong accent when he speaks. He has problems pronouncing words which begin in *w* or *wh*. He mispronounces *v* as an *f* and he has a very strong *s* sound. In addition he sometimes substitutes German words for English words.

5 Write the examples of Putz's speech below in standard English.

1 *Did you maybe try vashing der combustion chamber mit acid sulphuric? Sometimes der lead giffs a secondary radiation.*

2 *I bet it vas not serious.*

3 *Vot iss shenanigans?*

Both Putz and Leroy make grammatical mistakes when they speak. These are some of their mistakes:

1 They overuse the simple present when they should use the simple past or a continuous form.

2 Leroy in particular forgets the *s* on the third person singular.

3 Leroy has problems forming questions correctly.

4 Leroy often forgets articles.

6 Match the mistakes to the examples below and then correct the examples.

a) *Vas me! I hunt for you.*

b) *He is where?*

c) *He drink no water.*

d) *He is desert creature!*

e) *Why he rub his belly?*

f) *How you know?*

Main themes

Before you read the story, you may want to think about some of the main themes that occur. The questions will help you think about the story as you are reading it for the first time. There is more discussion of the main themes in the *Literary analysis* section after the story.

Martians

Martians in science-fiction stories before *The Martian Odyssey* were seen as aggressive invaders (for example in H G Wells' *The War of the Worlds*, 1898). They were enemies of the human race, technologically advanced and very dangerous. Man had to destroy them in order to save the planet.

7 As you read the story, think about these questions:

a) Are Weinbaum's Martians dangerous?

b) Are they a threat to humanity?

Understanding an alien culture

The main theme of the story is that of a meeting with an intelligent, alien life form. The main interest in the story is the relationship that develops between the alien, Tweel, and the astronaut, Jarvis.

8 As you read the story, think about these questions:

a) What is Jarvis's attitude to Tweel?
b) What is Tweel's attitude to Jarvis?
c) What is the basis for their friendship?

Measuring and judging intelligence

Another important theme is that of the nature of intelligence. Jarvis insists throughout his story that Tweel is an intelligent being, despite his co-astronauts' cynical responses.

9 As you read the story, think about these questions:

a) Is Tweel intelligent?
b) What about the other Martian creatures?
c) What signs of intelligence do they show?

The Martian Odyssey

by Stanley G Weinbaum

Jarvis stretched himself as luxuriously as he could in the **cramped** general quarters of the *Ares*.

"Air you can breathe!" he exulted. "It feels as thick as soup after the thin stuff out there!" He nodded at the Martian landscape stretching flat and **desolate** in the light of the nearer moon, beyond the glass of the port.

The other three stared at him sympathetically – Putz, the engineer, Leroy, the biologist, and Harrison, the astronomer and captain of the expedition. Dick Jarvis was chemist of the famous crew, the *Ares* expedition, first human beings to set foot on the mysterious neighbor[2] of the earth, the planet Mars. This, of course, was in the old days, less than twenty years after the mad American Doheny perfected the atomic blast at the cost of his life, and only a decade after the equally mad Cardoza rode on it to the moon. They were true pioneers, these four of the *Ares*. Except for a half-dozen moon expeditions and the ill-fated de Lancey flight aimed at the seductive orb of Venus, they were the first men to feel other gravity than earth's, and certainly the first successful crew to leave the earth-moon system. And they deserved that success when one considers the difficulties and discomforts – the months spent in acclimatization chambers back on earth, learning to breathe the air as **tenuous** as that of Mars, the challenging of the void in the tiny rocket driven by the **cranky**[3] reaction motors of the twenty-first century, and mostly the facing of an absolutely unknown world.

Jarvis stretched and fingered the raw and peeling tip of his **frostbitten** nose. He sighed again contentedly.

"Well," exploded Harrison abruptly, "are we going to hear what happened? You set out all **shipshape** in an auxiliary rocket,

2 *US spelling:* British spelling is *neighbour*
3 unreliable

we don't get a **peep** for ten days, and finally Putz here picks you out of a lunatic **ant-heap** with a **freak** ostrich as your **pal**! Spill it,[4] man!"

"Speel[5]?" queried Leroy perplexedly. "Speel what?"

"He means '*spiel*[6]," explained Putz soberly. "It iss to tell."

Jarvis met Harrison's amused glance without the shadow of a smile. "That's right, Karl," he said in grave agreement with Putz. "*Ich spiel es!*[7]" He grunted comfortably and began.

"According to orders," he said, "I watched Karl here take off toward the North, then I got into my flying sweat-box and headed south. You'll remember, Cap – we had orders not to land, but just **scout about** for points of interest. I set the two cameras clicking and **buzzed along**, riding pretty high – about two thousand feet – for a couple of reasons. First, it gave the cameras a greater field, and second, the under-jets[8] travel so far in this half-vacuum they call air here that they **stir up** dust if you move low."

"We know all that from Putz," grunted Harrison. "I wish you'd saved the films, though. They'd have paid the cost of this junket[9]; remember how the public mobbed[10] the first moon pictures?"

"The films are safe," retorted Jarvis. "Well," he resumed, "as I said, I buzzed along at a pretty good clip[11]; just as we figured, the wings haven't much lift in this air at less than a hundred miles per hour, and even then I had to use the under-jets.

"So, with the speed and the altitude and the blurring caused by the under-jets, the seeing wasn't any too good. I could see enough, though, to distinguish that what I sailed over was just more of this gray[12] **plain** that we'd been examining the whole week since our landing – same **blobby** growths and the same eternal carpet of crawling little plant-animals, or biopods[13], as

4 *informal:* to tell someone everything you know about something
5 imitating the pronunciation; he doesn't understand the word *spill*
6 *German:* tell
7 *German:* I'll tell it
8 the engines used to propel the rocket
9 *informal:* a journey or meeting people say is for business but is really for pleasure
10 *idiomatic:* got very excited about
11 *informal:* at a good speed
12 *US spelling:* British spelling is *grey*
13 two-legged creatures that are half-plant, half-animal, a term invented for the purposes of the story

Leroy calls them. So I sailed along, calling back my position every hour as instructed, and not knowing whether you heard me."

"I did!" snapped Harrison.

"A hundred and fifty miles south," continued Jarvis imperturbably, "the surface changed to a sort of low plateau, nothing but desert and orange-tinted sand. I figured that we were right in our guess, then, and this gray plain we dropped on was really the Mare Cimmerium which would make my orange desert the region called Xanthus. If I were right, I ought to hit another gray plain, the Mare Chronium in another couple of hundred miles, and then another orange desert, Thyle I or II. And so I did."

"Putz verified our position a week and a half ago!" grumbled the captain. "Let's get to the point."

"Coming!" remarked Jarvis. "Twenty miles into Thyle – believe it or not – I crossed a canal!"

"Putz photographed a hundred! Let's hear something new!"

"And did he also see a city?"

"Twenty of 'em, if you call those heaps of mud cities!"

"Well," observed Jarvis, "from here on I'll be telling a few things Putz didn't see!" He rubbed his tingling nose, and continued. "I knew that I had sixteen hours of daylight at this season, so eight hours – eight hundred miles – from here, I decided to turn back. I was still over Thyle, whether I or II I'm not sure, not more than twenty-five miles into it. And right there, Putz's pet motor **quit**!"

"Quit? How?" Putz was solicitous.

"The atomic blast got weak. I started losing altitude right away, and suddenly there I was with a thump right in the middle of Thyle! Smashed my nose on the window, too!" He rubbed the injured **member** ruefully.

"Did you maybe try vashing der combustion chamber mit acid sulphuric?" inquired Putz. "Sometimes der lead giffs a secondary radiation –"

"Naw!" said Jarvis disgustedly. "I wouldn't try that, of course – not more than ten times! Besides, the bump flattened the landing gear and busted[14] off the under-jets. Suppose I got the thing working – what then? Ten miles with the blast coming right out of the bottom and I'd have melted the floor from under me!" He rubbed his nose again. "Lucky for me a pound only weighs seven ounces here, or I'd have been mashed[15] flat!"

"I could have fixed!" ejaculated the engineer. "I bet it vas not serious."

"Probably not," agreed Jarvis sarcastically. "Only it wouldn't fly. Nothing serious, but I had the choice of waiting to be picked up or trying to walk back – eight hundred miles, and perhaps twenty days before we had to leave! Forty miles a day! Well," he concluded, "I chose to walk. Just as much chance of being picked up, and it kept me busy."

"We'd have found you," said Harrison.

"No doubt. Anyway, I **rigged up** a harness from some seat straps, and put the water tank on my back, took a cartridge belt and revolver, and some **iron rations**, and started out."

"Water tank!" exclaimed the little biologist, Leroy. "She weigh one-quarter ton!"

"Wasn't full. Weighed about two hundred and fifty pounds[16] earth-weight, which is eighty-five[17] here. Then, besides, my own personal two hundred and ten pounds[18] is only seventy[19] on Mars, so, tank and all, I grossed[20] a hundred and fifty-five[21], or fifty-five pounds[22] less than my everyday earth-weight. I figured on that when I undertook the forty-mile daily **stroll**. Oh – of course I took a thermo-skin sleeping bag for these wintry Martian nights.

"Off I went, bouncing along pretty quickly. Eight hours of daylight meant twenty miles or more. It got tiresome, of course – **plugging along** over a soft sand desert with nothing to see, not

14 *informal*: broke
15 crushed
16 114 kg
17 38 kg
18 95 kg
19 31 kg
20 came to a total of
21 70 kg
22 24 kg

even Leroy's crawling biopods. But an hour or so brought me to the canal – just a dry **ditch** about four hundred feet wide, and straight as a railroad on its own company map.

"There'd been water in it sometime, though. The ditch was covered with what looked like a nice green lawn. Only, as I approached, the lawn moved out of my way!"

"Eh?" said Leroy.

"Yeah, it was a relative of your biopods. I caught one, a little grass-like blade about as long as my finger, with two thin, stemmy legs."

"He is where?" Leroy was eager.

"He is let go! I had to move on, so I **plowed along**[23] with the walking grass opening in front and closing behind. And then I was out on the orange desert of Thyle again.

"I plugged steadily along, cussing[24] the sand that made going so tiresome, and, incidentally, cussing that cranky motor of yours, Karl. It was just before twilight that I reached the edge of Thyle, and looked down over the gray Mare Chronium. And I knew there was seventy-five miles of *that* to be walked over, and then a couple of hundred miles of that Xanthus desert, and about as much more Mare Cimmerium. Was I pleased? I started cussing you fellows for not picking me up!"

"We were trying, you sap[25]!" said Harrison.

"That didn't help. Well, I figured I might as well use what was left of daylight in getting down the cliff that bounded Thyle. I found an easy place, and down I went. Mare Chronium was just the same sort of place as this – crazy leafless plants and a bunch of crawlers; I gave it a glance and **hauled** out my sleeping bag. Up to that time, you know, I hadn't seen anything worth worrying about on this half-dead world – nothing dangerous, that is."

"Did you?" queried Harrison.

"*Did I!* You'll hear about it when I come to it. Well, I was

23 *US spelling:* British spelling is *ploughing*
24 *US, informal* (British: *curse*): to say or think offensive or impolite words about someone or something
25 fool

just about to turn in when suddenly I heard the wildest sort of shenanigans[26]!"

"Vot iss shenanigans?" inquired Putz.

"He says, '*Je ne sais quoi*,'" explained Leroy. "It is to say, 'I don't know what.'"

"That's right," agreed Jarvis. "I didn't know what, so I **sneaked** over to find out. There was a racket like a flock of crows eating a bunch of canaries – whistles, cackles, caws, trills, and what have you. I rounded a clump of stumps, and there was Tweel!"

"Tweel?" said Harrison, and "Tveel?" said Leroy and Putz.

"That freak ostrich," explained the narrator. "At least, Tweel is as near as I can pronounce it without **sputtering**. He called it something like 'Trrrweerrll!'."

"What was he doing?" asked the Captain.

"He was being eaten! And squealing, of course, as any one would."

"Eaten! By what?"

"I found out later. All I could see then was a bunch of black ropy arms **tangled** around what looked like, as Putz described it to you, an ostrich. I wasn't going to interfere, naturally; if both creatures were dangerous, I'd have one less to worry about.

"But the bird-like thing was putting up a good battle, dealing vicious blows with an eighteen-inch beak, between screeches. And besides, I caught a glimpse or two of what was on the end of those arms!" Jarvis **shuddered**. "But the **clincher** was when I noticed a little black bag or case hung about the neck of the bird-thing! It was intelligent. That or **tame**, I assumed. Anyway, it **clinched** my decision. I pulled out my automatic and fired into what I could see of its antagonist.

"There was a **flurry** of tentacles and a **spurt** of black **corruption**, and then the thing, with a disgusting sucking noise, pulled itself and its arms into a hole in the ground. The other let out a series of clacks, staggered around on legs about as thick as golf sticks, and turned suddenly to face me. I held my weapon ready, and the two of us stared at each other.

26 *informal*: high-spirited or mischievous activity

"The Martian wasn't a bird, really. It wasn't even bird-like, except just at first glance. It had a beak all right, and a few feathery appendages, but the beak wasn't really a beak. It was somewhat flexible; I could see the tip bend slowly from side to side; it was almost like a cross between a beak and a trunk. It had four-toed feet, and four-fingered things – hands, you'd have to call them, and a little roundish body, and a long neck ending in a tiny head – and that beak. It stood an inch or so taller than I, and – well, Putz saw it!"

The engineer nodded. "*Ja!* I saw!"

Jarvis continued. "So – we stared at each other. Finally the creature went into a series of clackings and twitterings and held out its hands toward me, empty. I took that as a gesture of friendship."

"Perhaps," suggested Harrison, "it looked at that nose of yours and thought you were its brother!"

"Huh! You can be funny without talking! Anyway, I put up my gun and said 'Aw, don't mention it,' or something of the sort, and the thing came over and we were pals.

"By that time, the sun was pretty low and I knew that I'd better build a fire or get into my thermo-skin. I decided on the fire. I picked a spot at the base of the Thyle cliff where the rock could reflect a little heat on my back. I started breaking off chunks of this desiccated[27] Martian vegetation, and my companion caught the idea and brought in an armful. I reached for a match, but the Martian fished into his **pouch** and brought out something that looked like a glowing coal; one touch of it, and the fire was blazing – and you all know what a job we have starting a fire in this atmosphere!

"And that bag of his!" continued the narrator. "That was a manufactured article, my friends; press an end and she[28] popped open – press the middle and she sealed so perfectly you couldn't see the line. Better than zippers[29].

---

27 *literary*: drier than it should be
28 the pronoun *she* can sometimes be used to talk about machines, though we normally prefer to use *it*
29 *US English*. British English: *zip*

"Well, we stared at the fire for a while and I decided to attempt some sort of communication with the Martian. I pointed at myself and said 'Dick'; he **caught the drift** immediately, stretched a bony claw at me and repeated 'Tick.' Then I pointed at him, and he gave that whistle I called Tweel; I can't imitate his accent. Things were going smoothly; to emphasize the names, I repeated 'Dick,' and then, pointing at him, 'Tweel.'

"There we stuck! He gave some clacks that sounded negative, and said something like 'P-p-p-root.' And that was just the beginning; I was always 'Tick,' but as for him – part of the time he was 'Tweel,' and part of the time he was 'P-p-p-proot,' and part of the time he was sixteen other noises!

"We just couldn't connect. I tried 'rock,' and I tried 'star,' and 'tree,' and 'fire' and Lord knows what else, and try as I would, I couldn't get a single word! Nothing was the same for two successive minutes, and if that's a language, I'm an alchemist. Finally I gave it up and called him Tweel, and that seemed to do.

"But Tweel hung on to some of my words. He remembered a couple of them, which I suppose is a great achievement if you're used to a language you have to make up as you go along. But I couldn't **get the hang of** his talk; either I missed some subtle point or we just didn't *think* alike – and I rather believe the latter view.

"I've other reasons for believing that. After a while I gave up the language business, and tried mathematics. I scratched two plus two equals four on the ground, and demonstrated it with pebbles. Again Tweel caught the idea, and informed me that three plus three equals six. Once more we seemed to be getting somewhere.

"So, knowing that Tweel had at least a grammar school education, I drew a circle for the sun, pointing first at it, and then at the last glow of the sun. Then I sketched in Mercury, and Venus, and Mother Earth, and Mars, and finally, pointing to Mars, I swept my hand around in a sort of inclusive gesture to indicate that Mars was our current environment. I was working up to putting over the idea that my home was on the earth.

"Tweel understood my diagram all right. He poked his beak at it, and with a great deal of trilling and clucking, he added Deimos and Phobos[30] to Mars, and then sketched in the earth's moon!

"Do you see what that proves? It proves that Tweel's race uses telescopes – that they're civilized!"

"Does not!" snapped Harrison. "The moon is visible from here as a fifth magnitude star[31]. They could see its revolution with the naked eye."

"The moon, yes!" said Jarvis. "You've missed my point. Mercury isn't visible! And Tweel knew of Mercury because he placed the Moon at the *third* planet, not the second. If he didn't know Mercury, he'd put the earth second, and Mars third, instead of fourth! See?"

"Humph!" said Harrison.

"Anyway," proceeded Jarvis, "I went on with my lesson. Things were going smoothly, and it looked as if I could put the idea over. I pointed at the earth on my diagram, and then at myself, and then, to clinch it, I pointed to myself and then to the earth itself shining bright green almost at the **zenith**.

"Tweel set up such an excited clacking that I was certain he understood. He jumped up and down, and suddenly he pointed at himself and then at the sky, and then at himself and at the sky again. He pointed at his middle and then at Arcturus, at his head and then at Spica, at his feet and then at half a dozen stars, while I just **gaped** at him. Then, all of a sudden, he gave a tremendous leap. Man, what a hop! He shot straight up into the starlight, seventy-five feet if an inch! I saw him silhouetted against the sky, saw him turn and come down at me head first, and land smack[32] on his beak like a javelin! There he stuck square in the centèr[33] of my sun-circle in the sand – a bull's eye[34]!"

30 the two moons of Mars
31 the brightness of stars is measured on a scale of magnitude. A fifth magnitude star is
    visible to the human eye without a telescope
32 *informal*: exactly in a particular place
33 *US spelling*: British spelling is *centre*
34 a shot or throw that hits the centre of a target

"Nuts!35" observed the Captain. "Plain nuts!"

"That's what I thought, too! I just stared at him openmouthed while he pulled his head out of the sand and stood up. Then I figured he'd missed my point, and I went through the whole **blamed rigmarole** again, and it ended the same way, with Tweel on his nose in the middle of my picture!"

"Maybe it's a religious rite," suggested Harrison.

"Maybe," said Jarvis dubiously. "Well, there we were. We could exchange ideas up to a certain point, and then – **blooey!** Something in us was different, unrelated; I don't doubt that Tweel thought me just as screwy36 as I thought him. Our minds simply looked at the world from different viewpoints, and perhaps his viewpoint is as true as ours. But – we couldn't get together, that's all. Yet, in spite of all difficulties, I *liked* Tweel, and I have a queer certainty that he liked me."

"Nuts!" repeated the captain. "Just daffy37!"

"Yeah? Wait and see. A couple of times I've thought that perhaps we – " He paused, and then resumed his narrative. "Anyway, I finally gave it up, and got into my thermo-skin to sleep. The fire hadn't kept me any too warm, but that damned sleeping bag did. Got **stuffy** five minutes after I closed myself in. I opened it a little and **bingo!** Some eighty-below-zero air hit my nose, and that's when I got this pleasant little frostbite to add to the bump I acquired during the crash of my rocket.

"I don't know what Tweel made of my sleeping. He sat around, but when I woke up, he was gone. I'd just crawled out of my bag, though, when I heard some twittering, and there he came, sailing down from that three-story Thyle cliff to **alight** on his beak beside me. I pointed to myself and toward the north, and he pointed at himself and toward the south, and when I loaded up and started away, he came along.

"Man, how he traveled38! A hundred and fifty feet at a jump, sailing through the air stretched out like a spear, and landing on his beak. He seemed surprised at my plodding, but after a

35 *informal:* crazy
36 *informal:* crazy
37 *informal:* crazy
38 US *spelling:* British spelling *travelled*

few moments he fell in beside me, only every few minutes he'd go into one of his leaps, and stick his nose into the sand a block ahead of me. Then he'd come shooting back at me; it made me nervous at first to see that beak of his coming at me like a spear, but he always ended in the sand at my side.

"So the two of us plugged along across the Mare Chronium. Same sort of place as this – same crazy plants and same little green biopods growing in the sand, or crawling out of your way. We talked – not that we understood each other, you know, but just for company. I sang songs, and I suspected Tweel did too; at least, some of his trillings and twitterings had a subtle sort of rhythm.

"Then, for variety, Tweel would display his **smattering** of English words. He'd point to an **outcropping** and say 'rock,' and point to a pebble and say it again; or he'd touch my arm and say 'Tick,' and then repeat it. He seemed terrifically amused that the same word meant the same thing twice in succession, or that the same word could apply to two different objects. It set me wondering if perhaps his language wasn't like the primitive speech of some earth people – you know, Captain, like the Negritoes[39], for instance, who haven't any generic words. No word for food or water or man – words for good food and bad food, or rainwater and seawater, or strong man and weak man – but no names for general classes. They're too primitive to understand that rain water and sea water are just different aspects of the same thing. But that wasn't the case with Tweel; it was just that we were somehow mysteriously different – our minds were alien to each other. And yet – we *liked* each other!"

"Looney[40], that's all," remarked Harrison. "That's why you two were so fond of each other."

"Well, I like *you*!" countered Jarvis wickedly. "Anyway," he resumed, "don't get the idea that there was anything screwy about Tweel. In fact, I'm not so sure but that he couldn't teach our highly praised human intelligence a trick or two. Oh, he

39 *old-fashioned*: a group of dark-skinned peoples of small stature that live in Oceania and the southeastern part of Asia
40 *informal*: crazy

wasn't an intellectual superman, I guess; but don't overlook the point that he managed to understand a little of my mental workings, and I never even got a glimmering of his."

"Because he didn't have any!" suggested the captain, while Putz and Leroy blinked attentively.

"You can judge of that when I'm through," said Jarvis. "Well, we plugged along across the Mare Chronium all that day, and all the next. Mare Chronium – Sea of Time! Say, I was willing to agree with Schiaparelli's name by the end of that march! Just that gray, endless plain of weird plants, and never a sign of any other life. It was so monotonous that I was even glad to see the desert of Xanthus toward the evening of the second day.

"I was fair worn out, but Tweel seemed as fresh as ever, for all I never saw him drink or eat. I think he could have crossed the Mare Chronium in a couple of hours with those block-long nose dives of his, but he stuck along with me. I offered him some water once or twice; he took the cup from me and sucked the liquid into his beak, and then carefully **squirted** it all back into the cup and gravely returned it.

"Just as we sighted Xanthus, or the cliffs that bounded it, one of those nasty sand clouds blew along, not as bad as the one we had here, but mean to travel against. I pulled the transparent flap of my thermo-skin bag across my face and managed pretty well, and I noticed that Tweel used some feathery appendages growing like a mustache[41] at the base of his beak to cover his nostrils, and some similar **fuzz** to shield his eyes."

"He is a desert creature!" ejaculated the little biologist, Leroy.

"Huh? Why?"

"He drink no water – he is adapt' for sand storm – "

"Proves nothing! There's not enough water to waste anywhere on this desiccated pill called Mars. We'd call all of it desert on earth, you know." He paused. "Anyway, after the sand storm blew over, a little wind kept blowing in our faces, not strong enough to stir the sand. But suddenly things came drifting along

41 US *spelling*: British spelling is *moustache*

from the Xanthus cliffs – small, transparent spheres, for all the world like glass tennis balls! But light – they were almost light enough to float even in this thin air – empty, too; at least, I cracked open a couple and nothing came out but a bad smell. I asked Tweel about them, but all he said was 'No, no, no,' which I took to mean that he knew nothing about them. So they went bouncing by like **tumbleweeds**, or like soap bubbles, and we plugged on toward Xanthus. Tweel pointed at one of the crystal balls once and said 'rock,' but I was too tired to argue with him. Later I discovered what he meant.

"We came to the bottom of the Xanthus cliffs finally, when there wasn't much daylight left. I decided to sleep on the **plateau** if possible; anything dangerous, I reasoned, would be more likely to prowl through the vegetation of the Mare Chronium than the sand of Xanthus. Not that I'd seen a single sign of menace, except the rope-armed black thing that had trapped Tweel, and apparently that didn't prowl at all, but lured its victims within reach. It couldn't lure me while I slept, especially as Tweel didn't seem to sleep at all, but simply sat patiently around all night. I wondered how the creature had managed to trap Tweel, but there wasn't any way of asking him. I found that out too, later; it's devilish!

"However, we were ambling around the base of the Xanthus barrier looking for an easy spot to climb. At least, I was. Tweel could have leaped it easily, for the cliffs were lower than Thyle – perhaps sixty feet. I found a place and started up, swearing at the water tank strapped to my back – it didn't bother me except when climbing – and suddenly I heard a sound that I thought I recognized!

"You know how deceptive sounds are in this thin air. A shot sounds like the pop of a cork. But this sound was the drone of a rocket, and sure enough, there went our second auxiliary about ten miles to westward, between me and the sunset!"

"Vas me!" said Putz. "I hunt for you."

"Yeah; I knew that, but what good did it do me? I hung on to the cliff and yelled and waved with one hand. Tweel saw it too, and set up a trilling and twittering, leaping to the top of the barrier and then high into the air. And while I watched, the machine droned on into the shadows to the south.

"I scrambled to the top of the cliff. Tweel was still pointing and trilling excitedly, shooting up toward the sky and coming down head-on to stick upside down on his back in the sand. I pointed toward the south, and at myself, and he said, 'Yes – Yes – Yes'; but somehow I gathered that he thought the flying thing was a relative of mine, probably a parent. Perhaps I did his intellect an injustice; I think now that I did.

"I was bitterly disappointed by the failure to attract attention. I pulled out my thermo-skin and crawled into it, as the night chill was already apparent. Tweel stuck his beak into the sand and drew up his legs and arms and looked for all the world like one of those leafless shrubs out there. I think he stayed that way all night."

"Protective **mimicry**!" ejaculated Leroy. "See? He is desert creature!"

"In the morning," resumed Jarvis, "we started off again. We hadn't gone a hundred yards into Xanthus when I saw something queer! This is one thing Putz didn't photograph, I'll wager!

"There was a line of little pyramids – tiny ones, not more than six inches high, stretching across Xanthus as far as I could see! Little buildings made of pygmy bricks, they were, hollow inside and truncated[42], or at least broken at the top and empty. I pointed at them and said 'What?' to Tweel, but he gave some negative twitters to indicate, I suppose, that he didn't know. So off we went, following the row of pyramids because they ran north, and I was going north.

"Man, we trailed that line for hours! After a while, I noticed another queer[43] thing: they were getting larger. Same number of bricks in each one, but the bricks were larger.

"By noon they were shoulder high. I looked into a couple – all just the same, broken at the top and empty. I examined a brick or two as well; they were silica, and old as creation itself!"

"How do you know?" asked Leroy.

42 *formal*: made shorter, especially by having the end or top removed
43 *old-fashioned*: strange

"They were weathered[44] – edges rounded. Silica doesn't weather easily even on earth, and in this climate –!"

"How old you think?"

"Fifty thousand – a hundred thousand years. How can I tell? The little ones we saw in the morning were older – perhaps ten times as old. Crumbling[45]. How old would that make *them*? Half a million years? Who knows?" Jarvis paused a moment. "Well," he resumed, "we followed the line. Tweel pointed at them and said 'rock' once or twice, but he'd done that many times before. Besides, he was more or less right about these.

"I tried questioning him. I pointed at a pyramid and asked 'People?' and indicated the two of us. He set up a negative sort of clucking and said, 'No, no, no. No one – one – two. No two – two – four,' meanwhile rubbing his stomach. I just stared at him and he went through the business again. 'No one – one – two. No two – two – four.' I just gaped at him."

"That proves it!" exclaimed Harrison. "Nuts!"

"You think so?" queried Jarvis sardonically. "Well, I figured it out different! 'No one – one – two!' You don't get it, of course, do you?"

"Nope[46] – nor do you!"

"I think I do! Tweel was using the few English words he knew to put over a very complex idea. What, let me ask, does mathematics make you think of?"

"Why – of astronomy. Or – or logic!"

"That's it! 'No one – one – two!' Tweel was telling me that the builders of the pyramids weren't people – or that they weren't intelligent, that they weren't reasoning creatures! Get it?"

"Huh! I'll be damned![47]"

"You probably will."

"Why," put in Leroy, "he rub his belly?"

"Why? Because, my dear biologist, that's where his brains are!

---

44 if something weathers or is weathered, its appearance changes because of the effect of wind, rain, etc

45 if a stone or brick crumbles, parts fall off because it is very old or damaged

46 *informal*: used for saying no when someone asks you a question

47 *informal* (possibly considered impolite): used for emphasising how surprised you are about something (literally, *damned* means sent to hell)

Not in his tiny head – in his middle!"

"C'est[48] *impossible!*"

"Not on Mars, it isn't! This flora and fauna aren't earthly; your biopods prove that!" Jarvis grinned and took up his narrative. "Anyway, we plugged along across Xanthus and in about the middle of the afternoon, something else queer happened. The pyramids ended."

"Ended!"

"Yeah; the queer part was that the last one – and now they were ten-footers – was capped! See? Whatever built it was still inside; we'd trailed 'em[49] from their half-million-year-old origin to the present.

"Tweel and I noticed it about the same time. I yanked out my automatic (I had a clip of Boland explosive bullets in it) and Tweel, quick as a sleight-of-hand[50] trick, snapped a queer little glass revolver out of his bag. It was much like our weapons, except that the grip[51] was larger to accommodate his four-taloned hand. And we held our weapons ready while we sneaked up along the lines of empty pyramids.

"Tweel saw the movement first. The top tiers of bricks were heaving, shaking, and suddenly slid down the sides with a thin crash. And then – something – something was coming out!

"A long, silvery-gray arm appeared, dragging after it an armored[52] body. Armored, I mean, with scales, silver-gray and dull-shining. *The arm* **heaved** the body out of the hole; the beast crashed to the sand.

"It was a **nondescript** creature – body like a big gray **cask**, arm and a sort of mouth-hole at one end; stiff, pointed tail at the other – and that's all. No other limbs, no eyes, ears, nose – nothing! The thing dragged itself a few yards, inserted its pointed tail in the sand, pushed itself upright, and just sat.

"Tweel and I watched it for ten minutes before it moved. Then, with a creaking and rustling like – oh, like crumpling stiff

48 *French*: it's/that's
49 *spoken*: them
50 clever and quick use of your hands, especially when performing a magic trick
51 the part of the gun that you hold in your hand
52 *US spelling*: British spelling is *armoured*

paper – its arm moved to the mouth-hole and out came a brick! The arm placed the brick carefully on the ground, and the thing was still again.

"Another ten minutes – another brick. Just one of Nature's bricklayers. I was about to slip away and move on when Tweel pointed at the thing and said 'rock'! I went 'huh?' and he said it again. Then, to the accompaniment of some of his trilling, he said, 'No – no – ' and gave two or three whistling breaths.

"Well, I got his meaning, for a wonder! I said, 'No breathe!' and demonstrated the word. Tweel was ecstatic; he said, 'Yes, yes, yes! No, no, no breet!' Then he gave a leap and sailed out to land on his nose about one pace from the monster!

"I was startled, you can imagine! The arm was going up for a brick, and I expected to see Tweel caught and **mangled**, but – nothing happened! Tweel **pounded** on the creature, and the arm took the brick and placed it neatly beside the first. Tweel **rapped** on its body again, and said 'rock', and I got up nerve enough to take a look myself.

"Tweel was right again. The creature *was* rock, and it didn't breathe!"

"How you know?" snapped Leroy, his black eyes blazing interest.

"Because I'm a chemist. The beast was made of silica! There must have been pure silicon in the sand, and it lived on that. Get it? We, and Tweel, and those plants out there, and even the biopods are *carbon* life; this thing lived by a different set of chemical reactions. It was silicon life!"

"*La vie silicieuse!*[53]" shouted Leroy. "I have suspect, and now it is proof! I must go see! *Il faut que je*[54] –"

"All right! All right!" said Jarvis. "You can go see. Anyhow, there the thing was, alive and yet not alive, moving every ten minutes, and then only to remove a brick. Those bricks were its waste matter. See, Frenchy? We're carbon, and our waste is carbon dioxide, and this thing is silicon and *its* waste is silicon dioxide – silica. But silica is a solid, hence the bricks. And it

53 *French*: silicon life
54 *French*: I must …

builds itself in, and when it is covered, it moves over to a fresh place to start over. No wonder it creaked! A living creature a half a million years old!"

"How you know how old?" Leroy was frantic.

"We trailed its pyramids from the beginning, didn't we? If this weren't the original pyramid builder, the series would have ended somewhere before we found him, wouldn't it? – ended and started over with the small ones. That's simple enough, isn't it?

"But he reproduces, or tries to. Before the third brick came out, there was a little rustle and out popped a whole stream of those little crystal balls. They're his **spores**, or seeds – call 'em what you want. They went bouncing by across Xanthus just as they'd bounced by us back in the Mare Chronium. I've a hunch[55] how they work, too – this is for your information, Leroy. I think the crystal shell of silica is no more than protective covering, like an eggshell, and that the active principle is the smell inside. It's some sort of gas that attacks silicon, and if the shell is broken near a supply of that element, some reaction starts that ultimately develops into a beast like that one."

"You should try!" exclaimed the little Frenchman. "We must break one to see!"

"Yeah? Well, I did. I smashed a couple against the sand. Would you like to come back in about ten thousand years to see if I planted some pyramid monsters? You'd most likely be able to tell by that time!" Jarvis paused and drew a deep breath. "Lord![56] That queer creature. Do you picture it? Blind, deaf, nerveless, brainless – just a mechanism, and yet – immortal! Bound to go on making bricks, building pyramids, as long as silicon and oxygen exist, and even afterwards it'll just stop. It won't be dead. If the accidents of a million years bring it its food again, there it'll be, ready to run again, while brains and civilizations are part of the past. A queer beast – yet I met a stranger one!"

"If you did, it must have been in your dreams!" growled Harrison.

55 a feeling that something is true, although you don't know any definite facts about it
56 an exclamation to show that you are surprised

"You're right!" said Jarvis soberly. "In a way, you're right. The dream-beast! That's the best name for it – and it's the most **fiendish**, terrifying creation one could imagine! More dangerous than a lion, more **insidious** than a snake!"

"Tell me!" begged Leroy. "I must go see!"

"Not *this* devil!" He paused again. "Well," he resumed, "Tweel and I left the pyramid creature and plowed along through Xanthus. I was tired and a little disheartened by Putz's failure to pick me up, and Tweel's trilling got on my nerves, as did his flying nosedives. So I just strode along without a word, hour after hour across that monotonous desert.

"Toward mid-afternoon we came in sight of a low dark line on the horizon. I knew what it was. It was a canal; I'd crossed it in the rocket and it meant that we were just one-third of the way across Xanthus. Pleasant thought, wasn't it? And still, I was keeping up to schedule.

"We approached the canal slowly; I remembered that this one was bordered by a wide fringe of vegetation and that Mudheap City was on it.

"I was tired, as I said. I kept thinking of a good hot meal, and then from that I jumped to reflections of how nice and home-like even Borneo would seem after this crazy planet, and from that, to thoughts of little old New York, and then to thinking about a girl I know there, Fancy Long. Know her?"

"Vision entertainer," said Harrison. "I've tuned her in. Nice blonde – dances and sings on the *Yerba Mate* hour."

"That's her," said Jarvis ungrammatically. "I know her pretty well – just friends, get me? – though she came down to see us off in the *Ares*. Well, I was thinking about her, feeling pretty lonesome[57], and all the time we were approaching that line of rubbery plants.

"And then – I said, 'What 'n[58] Hell!' and stared. And there she was – Fancy Long, standing plain as day under one of those crack-brained trees, and smiling and waving just the way I remembered her when we left!"

57 *US*: lonely
58 in

"Now you're nuts, too!" observed the captain.

"Boy, I almost agreed with you! I stared and pinched myself and closed my eyes and then stared again – and every time, there was Fancy Long smiling and waving! Tweel saw something, too; he was trilling and clucking away, but I scarcely heard him. I was bounding toward her over the sand, too amazed even to ask myself questions.

"I wasn't twenty feet from her when Tweel caught me with one of his flying leaps. He grabbed my arm, yelling, 'No – no – no!' in his squeaky voice. I tried to shake him off – he was as light as if he were built of bamboo – but he dug his claws in and yelled. And finally some sort of sanity returned to me and I stopped less than ten feet from her. There she stood, looking as solid as Putz's head!"

"Vot?" said the engineer.

"She smiled and waved, and waved and smiled, and I stood there dumb as Leroy, while Tweel squeaked and chattered. I *knew* it couldn't be real, yet – there she was!

"Finally I said, 'Fancy! Fancy Long!' She just kept on smiling and waving, but looking as real as if I hadn't left her thirty-seven million miles away.

"Tweel had his glass pistol out, pointing it at her. I grabbed his arm, but he tried to push me away. He pointed at her and said, 'No breet! No breet!' and I understood that he meant that the Fancy Long thing wasn't alive.

"Man, my head was whirling!

"Still, it gave me the **jitters** to see him pointing his weapon at her. I don't know why I stood there watching him take careful aim, but I did. Then he squeezed the handle of his weapon; there was a little puff of steam, and Fancy Long was gone! And in her place was one of those **writhing**, black rope-armed horrors like the one I'd saved Tweel from!

"The dream-beast! I stood there dizzy, watching it die while Tweel trilled and whistled. Finally he touched my arm, pointed at the twisting thing, and said, 'You one – one – two, he one – one – two.' After he'd repeated it eight or ten times, I got it. Do any of you?"

"Oui[59]," shrilled Leroy. "*Moi – je le comprends!*[60] He mean you think of something, the beast he know, and you see it! *Un chien*[61] – a hungry dog, he would see the big bone with meat! Or smell it – not?"

"Right!" said Jarvis. "The dream-beast uses its victim's **longings** and desires to trap its **prey**. The bird at nesting season would see its mate, the fox, prowling for its own prey, would see a helpless rabbit!"

"How he do?" queried Leroy.

"How do I know? How does a snake back on earth charm a bird into its very jaws? And aren't there deep-sea fish that lure their victims into their mouths? Lord!" Jarvis shuddered. "Do you see how insidious the monster is? We're warned now – but henceforth[62] we can't trust even our eyes. You might see me – I might see one of you – and back of it[63] may be nothing but another of those black horrors!"

"How'd your friend know?" asked the captain abruptly.

"Tweel? I wonder! Perhaps he was thinking of something that couldn't possibly have interested me, and when I started to run, he realized that I saw something different and was warned. Or perhaps the dream-beast can only project a single vision, and Tweel saw what I saw – or nothing. I couldn't ask him. But it's just another proof that his intelligence is equal to ours or greater."

"He's daffy, I tell you!" said Harrison. "What makes you think his intellect ranks with the human?"

"Plenty of things! First the pyramid-beast. He hadn't seen one before; he said as much. Yet he recognized it as a dead-alive automaton of silicon."

"He could have heard of it," objected Harrison. "He lives around here, you know."

"Well how about the language? I couldn't pick up a single idea of his and he learned six or seven words of mine. And do you

59 *French:* yes
60 *French:* me – I understand
61 *French:* a dog
62 *formal:* from this time into the future
63 *US English:* British English is *behind it*

realize what complex ideas he put over with no more than those six or seven words? The pyramid monster – the dream-beast! In a single phrase he told me that one was a harmless automaton and the other a deadly hypnotist. What about that?"

"Huh!" said the captain.

"*Huh* if you wish! Could you have done it knowing only six words of English? Could you go even further, as Tweel did, and tell me that another creature was of a sort of intelligence so different from ours that understanding was impossible – even more impossible than that between Tweel and me?"

"Eh? What was that?"

"Later. The point I'm making is that Tweel and his race are worthy of our friendship. Somewhere on Mars – and you'll find I'm right – is a civilization and culture equal to ours, and maybe more than equal. And communication is possible between them and us; Tweel proves that. It may take years of patient trial, for their minds are alien, but less alien than the next minds we encountered – if they *are* minds."

"The next ones? What next ones?"

"The people of the mud cities along the canals." Jarvis frowned, then resumed his narrative. "I thought the dream-beast and the silicon-monster were the strangest beings conceivable, but I was wrong. These creatures are still more alien, less understandable than either and far less comprehensible than Tweel, with whom friendship is possible, and even, by patience and concentration, the exchange of ideas.

"Well," he continued, "we left the dream-beast dying, dragging itself back into its hole, and we moved toward the canal. There was a carpet of that queer walking-grass scampering out of our way, and when we reached the bank, there was a yellow trickle of water flowing. The mound city I'd noticed from the rocket was a mile or so to the right and I was curious enough to want to take a look at it.

"It had seemed deserted from my previous glimpse of it and if any creatures were lurking in it – well, Tweel and I were both armed. And by the way, that crystal weapon of Tweel's was an interesting device; I took a look at it after the dream-beast episode. It fired a little glass splinter, poisoned, I suppose, and I guess it held at least a hundred of 'em to a load. The propellant was steam – just plain steam!"

"Shteam!" echoed Putz. "From vot come, shteam?"

"From water, of course! You could see the water through the transparent handle and about a gill[64] of another liquid, thick and yellowish. When Tweel squeezed the handle – there was no trigger – a drop of water and a drop of the yellow stuff squirted into the firing chamber, and the water vaporized – pop! – like that. It's not so difficult; I think we could develop the same principle. Concentrated sulfuric acid will heat water almost to boiling, and so will quicklime[65], and there's potassium and sodium –

"Of course, his weapon hadn't the range of mine, but it wasn't so bad in this thin air, and it *did* hold as many shots as a cowboy's gun in a Western movie. It was effective, too, at least against Martian life; I tried it out, aiming at one of the crazy plants, and darned[66] if the plant didn't **wither** up and fall apart! That's why I think the glass splinters were poisoned.

"Anyway, we trudged along toward the mud-heap city and I began to wonder whether the city builders dug the canals. I pointed to the city and then at the canal, and Tweel said 'No – no – no!' and gestured toward the south. I took it to mean that some other race had created the canal system, perhaps Tweel's people. I don't know; maybe there's still another intelligent race on the planet, or a dozen others. Mars is a queer little world.

"A hundred yards from the city we crossed a sort of road – just a hard-packed mud trail, and then, all of a sudden, along came one of the mound builders!

"Man, talk about fantastic beings! It looked rather like a barrel trotting along on four legs with four other arms or tentacles. It had no head, just body and members and a row of eyes completely around it. The top end of the barrel-body was a

64 a unit for measuring liquid equal to 4 fluid ounces (roughly 120 ml)
65 a form of calcium oxide (CaO)
66 US: short for *I'll be darned*, an alternative form of *I'll be damned*, used for emphasising how surprised you are

diaphragm stretched as tight as a drumhead, and that was all. It was pushing a little coppery cart and tore right past us like the proverbial bat out of Hell[67]. It didn't even notice us, although I thought the eyes on my side shifted a little as it passed.

"A moment later another came along, pushing another empty cart. Same thing – it just scooted past us. Well, I wasn't going to be ignored by a bunch of barrels playing train, so when the third one approached, I planted myself in the way – ready to jump, of course, if the thing didn't stop.

"But it did. It stopped and set up a sort of drumming from the diaphragm on top. And I held out both hands and said, 'We are friends!' And what do you suppose the thing did?"

"Said, 'Pleased to meet you,' I'll bet!" suggested Harrison.

"I couldn't have been more surprised if it had! It drummed on its **diaphragm**, and then suddenly boomed out, 'We are v-r-r-riends' and gave its pushcart a vicious poke at me! I jumped aside, and away it went while I stared dumbly after it.

"A minute later another one came hurrying along. This one didn't pause, but simply drummed out, 'We are v-r-r-riends!' and scurried by. How did it learn the phrase? Were all of the creatures in some sort of communication with each other? Were they all parts of some central organism? I don't know, though I think Tweel does.

"Anyway, the creatures went sailing past us, every one greeting us with the same statement. It got to be funny; I never thought to find so many friends on this God-forsaken ball! Finally I made a puzzled gesture to Tweel; I guess he understood, for he said, 'One-one-two – yes! – Two-two-four – no!' Get it?"

"Sure," said Harrison. "It's a Martian nursery rhyme."

"Yeah! Well, I was getting used to Tweel's symbolism, and I figured it out this way. 'One-one-two – yes!' The creatures were intelligent. 'Two-two-four – no!' Their intelligence was not of our order, but something different and beyond the logic of two and two is four. Maybe I missed his meaning. Perhaps he meant that their minds were of low degree, able to figure out the simple

---

67   referrring to the proverb *like a bat out of Hell*, meaning very fast

things – 'One-one-two – yes!' – but not more difficult things – 'Two-two-four – no!' But I think from what we saw later that he meant the other.

"After a few moments, the creatures came rushing back – first one, then another. Their pushcarts were full of stones, sand, chunks of rubbery plants, and such rubbish as that. They droned out their friendly greeting, which didn't really sound so friendly, and dashed on. The third one I assumed to be my first acquaintance and I decided to have another chat with him. I stepped into his path again and waited.

"Up he came, booming out his 'We are v-r-r-riends' and stopped. I looked at him; four or five of his eyes looked at me. He tried his password again and gave a shove on his cart, but I stood firm. And then the – the dashed[68] creature reached out one of his arms, and two finger-like nippers[69] tweaked my nose!"

"Haw!" roared Harrison. "Maybe the things have a sense of beauty!"

"Laugh!" grumbled Jarvis. "I'd already had a nasty bump and a mean frostbite on that nose. Anyway, I yelled 'Ouch!' and jumped aside and the creature dashed away; but from then on, their greeting was 'We are v-r-r-riends! Ouch!' Queer beasts!

"Tweel and I followed the road squarely up to the nearest mound. The creatures were coming and going, paying us not the slightest attention, fetching their loads of rubbish. The road simply dived into an opening, and slanted down like an old mine, and in and out darted the barrel-people, greeting us with their eternal phrase.

"I looked in; there was a light somewhere below, and I was curious to see it. It didn't look like a flame or torch, you understand, but more like a civilized light, and I thought that I might get some clue as to the creatures' development. So in I went and Tweel tagged along, not without a few trills and twitters, however.

"The light was curious; it sputtered and flared like an old **arc light**, but came from a single black rod set in the wall of the

68 *old-fashioned, informal*: an alternative form of *damned*, used for expressing annoyance
69 pincers, like the claws on crab or lobster

corridor. It was electric, beyond doubt. The creatures were fairly civilized, apparently.

"Then I saw another light shining on something that glittered and I went on to look at that, but it was only a heap of shiny sand. I turned toward the entrance to leave, and the Devil take me if it wasn't gone!

"I supposed the corridor had curved, or I'd stepped into a side passage. Anyway, I walked back in that direction I thought we'd come, and all I saw was more dimlit corridor. The place was a **labyrinth**! There was nothing but twisting passages running every way, lit by occasional lights, and now and then a creature running by, sometimes with a pushcart, sometimes without.

"Well, I wasn't much worried at first. Tweel and I had only come a few steps from the entrance. But every move we made after that seemed to get us in deeper. Finally I tried following one of the creatures with an empty cart, thinking that he'd be going out for his rubbish, but he ran around aimlessly, into one passage and out another. When he started dashing around a pillar like one of these Japanese waltzing mice[70], I gave up, dumped my water tank on the floor, and sat down.

"Tweel was as lost as I. I pointed up and he said 'No – no – no!' in a sort of helpless trill. And we couldn't get any help from the natives. They paid no attention at all, except to assure us they were friends – ouch!

"Lord! I don't know how many hours or days we wandered around there! I slept twice from sheer exhaustion; Tweel never seemed to need sleep. We tried following only the upward corridors, but they'd run uphill a ways[71] and then curve downwards. The temperature in that damned ant hill was constant; you couldn't tell night from day and after my first sleep I didn't know whether I'd slept one hour or thirteen, so I couldn't tell from my watch whether it was midnight or noon.

"We saw plenty of strange things. There were machines running in some of the corridors, but they didn't seem to be doing anything – just wheels turning. And several times I saw

70 an Asian breed of mice, so called because of their habit of running in circles
71 US, *informal*: for a time

two barrel-beasts with a little one growing between them, joined to both."

"Parthenogenesis[72]!" exulted Leroy. "Parthenogenesis by budding[73] like *les tulipes*[74]!"

"If you say so, Frenchy," agreed Jarvis. "The things never noticed us at all, except, as I say, to greet us with 'We are v-r-r-riends! Ouch!' They seemed to have no home-life of any sort, but just scurried around with their pushcarts, bringing in rubbish. And finally I discovered what they did with it.

"We'd had a little luck with a corridor, one that slanted upwards for a great distance. I was feeling that we ought to be close to the surface when suddenly the passage debouched[75] into a domed chamber, the only one we'd seen. And man! – I felt like dancing when I saw what looked like daylight through a **crevice** in the roof.

"There was a – a sort of machine in the chamber, just an enormous wheel that turned slowly, and one of the creatures was in the act of dumping his rubbish below it. The wheel **ground** it with a crunch – sand, stones, plants, all into powder that **sifted** away somewhere. While we watched, others filed in, repeating the process, and that seemed to be all. No rhyme nor reason to the whole thing – but that's characteristic of this crazy planet. And there was another fact that's almost too bizarre to believe.

"One of the creatures, having dumped his load, pushed his cart aside with a crash and calmly shoved himself under the wheel! I watched him being crushed, too stupefied to make a sound, and a moment later, another followed him! They were perfectly methodical about it, too; one of the cartless creatures took the abandoned pushcart.

"Tweel didn't seem surprised; I pointed out the next suicide to him, and he just gave the most human-like shrug imaginable, as

72 a form of asexual reproduction. The term does not match current, scientific use, as only one parent is needed for parthenogenesis to take place.

73 to produce a bud is when a part of a living thing grows from it before separating and becoming a new organism

74 *French*: tulips – a large, colourful flower shaped like a cup that grows on a long stem in spring

75 *formal*: to move or turn into an open space

much as to say, 'What can I do about it?' He must have known more or less about these creatures.

"Then I saw something else. There was something beyond the wheel, something shining on a sort of low **pedestal**. I walked over; there was a little crystal, about the size of an egg, fluorescing to beat Tophet[76]. The light from it stung my hands and face, almost like a static discharge, and then I noticed another funny thing. Remember that **wart** I had on my left thumb? Look!" Jarvis extended his hand. "It dried up and fell off – just like that! And my abused nose – say, the pain went out of it like magic! The thing had the property of hard ex-rays or gamma radiations, only more so; it destroyed diseased tissue and left healthy tissue unharmed!

"I was thinking what a present *that'd* be to take back to Mother Earth when a lot of racket interrupted. We dashed back to the other side of the wheel in time to see one of the pushcarts ground up. Some suicide had been careless, it seems.

"Then suddenly the creatures were booming and drumming all around us and their noise was decidedly menacing. A crowd of them advanced toward us; we backed out of what I thought was the passage we'd entered by, and they came rumbling after us, some pushing carts and some not. Crazy brutes! There was a whole chorus of 'We are v-r-r-riends! Ouch!' I didn't like the 'ouch'; it was rather suggestive.

"Tweel had his glass gun out and I dumped my water tank for greater freedom and got mine. We backed up the corridor with the barrel-beasts following – about twenty of them. Queer thing – the ones coming in with loaded carts moved past us inches away without a sign.

"Tweel must have noticed that. Suddenly, he snatched out that glowing coal cigar-lighter of his and touched a cartload of plant limbs. Puff! The whole load was burning – and the crazy beast pushing it went right along without a change of pace. It created some disturbance among our 'v-v-r-riends', however

76 believed to be a location in Jerusalem where fires were continually burning carcasses and animal waste

– and then I noticed the smoke eddying[77] and swirling past us, and sure enough, there was the entrance!

"I grabbed Tweel and out we dashed and after us our twenty pursuers. The daylight felt like Heaven, though I saw at first glance that the sun was all but set, and that was bad, since I couldn't live outside my thermo-skin bag in a Martian night – at least, without a fire.

"And things got worse in a hurry. They cornered us in an angle between two mounds, and there we stood. I hadn't fired, nor had Tweel; there wasn't any use in irritating the brutes. They stopped a little distance away and began their booming about friendship and ouches.

"Then things got still worse! A barrel-brute came out with a pushcart and they all grabbed into it and came out with handfuls of foot-long copper darts – sharp-looking ones – and all of a sudden one sailed past my ear – zing! And it was shoot or die then.

"We were doing pretty well for a while. We picked off the ones next to the pushcart and managed to keep the darts at a minimum, but suddenly there was a thunderous booming of 'v-v-r-riends' and 'ouches', and a whole army of 'em came out of their hole.

"Man! We were through and I knew it! Then I realized that Tweel wasn't. He could have leaped the mound behind us as easily as not. He was staying for me!

"Say, I could have cried if there'd been time! I'd liked Tweel from the first, but whether I'd have had gratitude to do what he was doing – suppose I *had* saved him from the first dream-beast – he'd done as much for me, hadn't he? I grabbed his arm, and said 'Tweel,' and pointed up, and he understood. He said, 'No – no – no, Tick!' and popped away with his glass pistol.

"What could I do? I'd be a goner[78] anyway when the sun set, but I couldn't explain that to him. I said, 'Thanks, Tweel. You're a man!' and felt that I wasn't paying him any compliment at all. A man! There are mighty few men who'd do that.

77 move in a circular pattern
78 *informal*: someone who is sure to die soon

"So I went 'bang' with my gun and Tweel went 'puff' with his, and the barrels were throwing darts and getting ready to rush us, and booming about being friends. I had given up hope. Then suddenly an angel dropped right down from Heaven in the shape of Putz, with his underjets blasting the barrels into very small pieces!

"Wow! I let out a yell and dashed for the rocket; Putz opened the door and in I went, laughing and crying and shouting! It was a moment or so before I remembered Tweel; I looked around in time to see him rising in one of his nosedives over the mound and away.

"I had a devil of a job arguing Putz into following! By the time we got the rocket aloft, darkness was down; you know how it comes here – like turning off a light. We sailed out over the desert and put down once or twice. I yelled 'Tweel!' and yelled it a hundred times, I guess. We couldn't find him; he could travel like the wind and all I got – or else I imagined it – was a faint trilling and twittering drifting out of the south. He'd gone, and damn it! I wish – I wish he hadn't!"

The four men of the *Ares* were silent – even the sardonic Harrison. At last little Leroy broke the stillness.

"I should like to see," he murmured.

"Yeah," said Harrison. "And the wart-cure. Too bad you missed that; it might be the cancer cure they've been hunting for a century and a half."

"Oh, that!" muttered Jarvis gloomily. "That's what started the fight!" He drew a glistening object from his pocket.

"Here it is."

Post-reading exercises

Understanding the story

1 **Use these questions to help you check that you have understood the story.**

1 How many men are there on the *Ares*?
2 What's special about them?
3 How long has Jarvis been away from the rest of the crew?
4 Why do Leroy and Putz have problems understanding Jarvis and Harrison?
5 What was Jarvis's mission?
6 Why did he decide to turn back?
7 What happened to the rocket's motor?
8 What happened to Jarvis's nose?
9 Why did he decide to walk?
10 What equipment did he take with him? Why?
11 Where did he decide to stop for the night? Why?
12 Why did he decide to help Tweel?
13 How did Tweel show that he wanted to thank Jarvis?
14 How did Tweel light the fire?
15 Why was this so impressive?
16 Why was Jarvis interested in Tweel's bag?
17 What were Jarvis's first attempts at communication?
18 Were they successful?
19 Who had more success, Jarvis or Tweel? Why?
20 What was strange about the way Tweel moved?
21 Why did Tweel go with Jarvis?
22 What conclusions did Jarvis draw about Tweel and his language?
23 How long did it take them to cross the Mare Chronium? How did they both feel by the time they reached Xanthus?
24 How did they protect themselves against the sandstorm?
25 What was Tweel's reaction to Putz's rocket? What did it mean?
26 Why did they follow the pyramids? How did the pyramids change as they followed them?
27 How did Jarvis calculate the age of the pyramids?
28 What did Tweel tell Jarvis about them? How did Jarvis work out the message?
29 What came out of the last pyramid?
30 How did it produce the bricks?
31 How did the creatures reproduce?

32 What was Jarvis thinking of as he approached the canal?
33 What did he think he saw?
34 How did Tweel save him?
35 What does Jarvis claim this shows about Tweel and his civilisation?
36 What were the creatures of the mud cities like?
37 What were they doing?
38 Why did they all imitate Jarvis when he said *We are friends*?
39 Why did Jarvis follow them into the tunnel?
40 What made him think the barrel people were civilised?
41 How long did they stay in the tunnel?
42 What did the barrel creatures do with the rubbish in their carts?
43 What did Jarvis see behind the machine?
44 Why did the barrel creatures suddenly attack Jarvis and Tweel?
45 How did they both eventually escape?
46 What has Jarvis got in his pocket?
47 Why didn't he mention it earlier?

Language study

A large part of the story is dedicated to describing the strange habits
of the creatures Jarvis meets on Mars. In these descriptions, Jarvis
often uses comparisons to help him describe the details of his story as
clearly as possible to his fellow astronauts. The structure he uses most
frequently is *as … as …*

as … as …

Form

The most common form is **as + adjective + as + noun**, eg

 as thick as soup

But other forms are also possible.

as	adjective adverb *much/many* + noun	*as*	noun clause adverb (eg *ever/not*)

Here are some examples from the story:

as + adj + as + clause
I don't doubt that Tweel thought me as screwy as I thought him.

as + adj + as + adv
I was fair worn out, but Tweel seemed as fresh as ever.

as + many + noun + as + noun
It did hold as many shots as a cowboy's gun in a Western movie.

as + adv + as + adv
He could have leaped the mound behind us as easily as not.

Use

We use *as … as …* to compare two objects, people, places or events and to say that they are very similar.

1 Complete the extracts below with the words in the box to form comparisons.

light   long   solid   thick   tight   true

1   *I caught one, a little grass-like blade about as .... as my finger.*
2   *The other … staggered around on legs about as .... as golf sticks.*
3   *Perhaps his viewpoint is as .... as ours.*
4   *He was as .... as if he were built of bamboo.*
5   *There she stood, looking as .... as Putz's head.*
6   *The top end of the barrel-body was a diaphragm stretched as ....
    as a drumhead.*

Continuous aspect

Throughout the story Jarvis uses continuous forms to set the scene and to describe the strange actions the creatures are performing.

Form

Continuous verb forms are formed by using the verb *be* + *-ing*. The verb *be* can be in any form. Here are some examples.

Present: *is/are* + *-ing*

The point I'm making is that Tweel and his race are worthy of our friendship.

Present perfect: *has/have been* + *-ing*

The cancer cure they've been hunting for a century and a half.

Past: *was/were + -ing*

He **was thinking** *of something that couldn't possibly have interested me.*

Past perfect: *had been + -ing*

More of this gray plain that we'd been examining the whole week.

Future: *will be + -ing*

I'll be telling a few things Putz didn't see!

Use

We use continuous forms to show that an action *is/was/is going to be* **in progress** at a given point in time.

action in progress

————————————————————————— X ————————————————————————————

point in time

2 **Look at these examples. Underline the continuous form in each example and answer the questions below.**

1 *Things were going smoothly; to emphasize the names, I repeated 'Dick,' and then, pointing at him, 'Tweel.'*

2 *We were ambling around the base of the Xanthus barrier looking for an easy spot to climb.*

3 *After a while, I noticed another queer thing: they were getting larger.*

– What tense is the verb *be*?

– This is the form that is used most frequently in the story. Why do you think that is?

– In which example is the continuous form:

   a) describing an action in progress?

   b) describing a situation that is changing over time?

   c) describing the longer of two actions?

3 **Complete the extracts below with the past continuous form of the verbs in the box.**

approach go pay stay tell think use

1 *Tweel .... the few English words he knew to put over a very complex idea.*

2 *Tweel .... me that the builders of the pyramids weren't people – or that they weren't intelligent, that they weren't reasoning creatures!*

3 *The arm .... up for a brick, and I expected to see Tweel caught and mangled.*

4 *Well, I* .... *about her, feeling pretty lonesome, and all the time we* .... *that line of rubbery plants.*

5 *He* .... *for me!*

6 *I said 'Thanks, Tweel. You're a man!' and felt that I* .... *him any compliment at all.*

4 Write the verbs in brackets in an appropriate continuous form.

1 This time next week we .... (arrive) back on Earth.

2 We .... (work) hard on this project now for the last ten months.

3 He ....(walk) for five days non-stop and he was exhausted.

4 What I .... (try) to tell you is that he had become my best friend.

5 We .... (cross) the last few miles of the red desert when we heard a strange noise.

6 I don't know what he's doing. I suppose he .... (might/look) for food.

Omitting the verb *be*

– when using *and* to combine sentences

Sometimes we can combine two or more verbs in one sentence by using *and* and omitting the subject and the verb *be*.

Look at this example. Notice how three separate sentences have been combined into one.

The barrels were throwing darts and getting ready to rush us, and booming about being friends.

1 The barrels were throwing darts.
2 They were getting ready to rush us.
3 They were booming about being friends.

5 Now look at these sentences. Combine the three sentences into one using *and* where necessary and dropping any unnecessary words.

1 The creatures were coming and they were going.
2 They were paying us not the slightest attention.
3 They were fetching their loads of rubbish.

= ───

– in relative clauses

We can also omit the verb *be* in a relative clause when the relative pronoun is the subject of the relative clause.

Look at these examples:

I wasn't going to be ignored by a bunch of barrels (~~which were~~) playing train.

He was watching the man (~~who was~~) standing behind me.

6 Look at these extracts. What words have been omitted in the positions marked by an asterisk *?

1 *And there she was – Fancy Long, * standing plain as day under one of those crack-brained trees, and * smiling and * waving just the way I remembered her when we left!*

2 *A long, silvery-gray arm appeared, * dragging after it an armored body.*

3 *Tweel was still pointing and * trilling excitedly, * shooting up toward the sky and * coming down head-on to stick upside down on his beak in the sand.*

4 *The bird-like thing was putting up a good battle, * dealing vicious blows with an eighteen-inch beak.*

5 *'What was he doing?' asked the Captain.*
  'He was being eaten. And * squealing, of course, as anyone would.'

6 *Several times I saw two barrel-beasts with a little one * growing between them.*

7 *I pointed to myself and then to the earth itself * shining bright green.*

8 *I noticed that Tweel used some feathery appendages * growing like a mustache at the base of his beak to cover his nostrils.*

Literary analysis

Plot

1 The plot is fairly simple. It follows Jarvis's trek across Mars, until he is finally picked up by his co-astronaut, Putz. Here are the main events. Put them in the correct order.
   a) Jarvis's rocket crashed
   b) Jarvis was taking pictures of Mars
   c) Jarvis saw a dream beast for the first time
   d) The barrel-beasts attacked Jarvis
   e) The dream beast tried to lure Jarvis into his tentacles
   f) Tweel pulled out his steam gun for the first time
   g) Jarvis picked up the magic crystal
   h) Putz saved Jarvis
   i) Tweel saved Jarvis
   j) Jarvis saved Tweel

2 Which do you think is the most important event? Why? Write a one-sentence summary of the plot.

3 Is the story told in the same sequence as it happened? When does the story start?

4 What is the story really about: the strange creatures of Mars, Tweel, Jarvis or something else?

Characters

5 What do we know about Jarvis? What do we know about Tweel? Describe the relationship between them.

6 Which character do you sympathise with most? Why? Which of the two do you think is:
   a) more intelligent?
   b) more generous in his friendship?
   Justify your answers.

7 What do you know about the other three men on board the *Ares*? What are their different roles, on the mission, and what are their roles in the story?

8 Think about the other Martian creatures Jarvis meets. What do they represent? Which do you think is the most interesting? Why?

9 Think about Tweel. Think about his gun, his initial gesture of thanks, his knowledge of the planets, the way he moves, the way he talks, what he eats and drinks. In what ways is he similar to humans, and in what ways is he different?

10 It has been said that Weinbaum was possibly the first science-fiction writer to describe an alien 'who thinks *as well as* a man, or *better* than a man, but not *like* a man.'[79] To what extent do you think this is true of Tweel?

Narration

11 How does the story begin? Who is the narrator?
12 Jarvis tells his story in his own words, interrupted at times by his co-astronauts. How do their interruptions help to shape the story? What are the crew members interested in finding out?
13 What is the crew's reaction to Tweel? How does this affect the way Jarvis describes him?
14 If Jarvis had written his story in a diary, without the interruptions and comments of his friends, how might it have been different?

Style

15 Jarvis's narrative is told in an informal, chatty style. What are the main features of Jarvis's story-telling style? How does his relationship with the rest of the crew influence his style?
16 When he describes the geography of Mars and the strange creature he sees, he doesn't use scientific and technical terms, but compares the creatures to common, everyday things back home on Earth. Look at the comparisons below. Underline the everyday objects he chooses for his comparisons.
    a) *But an hour or so brought me to the canal – just a dry ditch about four hundred feet wide, and straight as a railroad on its own company map.*
    b) *The ditch was covered with what looked like a nice green lawn. Only, as I approached, the lawn moved out of my way!*
    c) *There was a racket like a flock of crows eating a bunch of canaries.*
    Find other similar comparisons (for example when he talks about the mudheap cities and the barrel-shaped creatures).
    What is the overall effect of these comparisons? Why do you think Jarvis likes to make these kinds of comparisons? What does it tell us about him and his experience?
17 Jarvis and the rest of the crew give the Martians nick-names: the freak ostrich, the dream beasts, the pyramid monsters and the

79 John W Campbell, an influential science-fiction editor during the Golden Age of Science Fiction in the 1930s to 1950s

barrel-beasts. What is the effect created by this? What does it tell us about the crew members and their relationship with each other?

18 Look at the closing paragraphs of the story. Jarvis's tone has become far more serious. Why? What is his main concern at the end? And what is Harrison's?

Guidance to the above literary terms, answer keys to all the exercises and activities, plus a wealth of other reading-practice material, can be found on the student's section of the Macmillan Readers website at: www.macmillanenglish.com/readers.

The Shadow and the Flash

by Jack London

About the author

Jack London was a US author. He was also an adventurer and a man of action. In his short life he was a sailor, a tramp and a gold digger, as well as a prolific writer. He wrote 19 novels and almost 200 short stories. He was one of the first Americans to make a career exclusively from writing and became the highest-paid writer of his time. He is best known for his novels, *The Call of the Wild*, *White Fang* and *The Sea Wolf*.

Jack London was born in San Francisco in 1876. It is not clear who his father was, and London's birth certificate was lost when most of the San Francisco civil records of the time were lost in the great fires that followed the 1906 San Francisco earthquake.

He was brought up by his mother, Flora Wellman, and an ex-slave, Virginia Prentiss. He came from a poor, working-class background and mainly educated himself by reading books in the public library. He started working when he was ten, selling newspapers on the street. Over the next 14 years he had a string of different jobs. He worked in a canning factory, in a laundry and in a power station. He spent periods of time living like a tramp, on the street, without a job and was at one point sent to prison for 30 days for vagrancy (living on the streets). He also worked as an oyster pirate (stealing oysters at night to sell illegally) and a sailor, and travelled to Alaska in search of gold.

In 1898, he returned from Alaska to his hometown of Oakland and began a three-year battle to make a living as a writer. London was lucky that at the time he started writing, new printing technology was making the production of low-cost magazines possible for the first time, and this brought with it a strong market for short stories. In 1900, London made over $2,500 from writing, the equivalent of roughly $200,000 today. In 1903, Macmillan bought the rights to the now classic story *The Call of the Wild* for $2,000. It was through their promotion of the story that London's name first became so well known.

In 1905, London was in San Francisco to witness the great earthquake that destroyed a great part of the city. He published an eye-witness report of the earthquake and the fires that followed in the *Collier* magazine. It is said that he was also responsible for helping to save hundreds of lives as he carried children to safety from their burning homes.

In 1910, he bought a ranch in Sonoma County, California, and in the years that followed, he became more and more interested in developing and managing the ranch. His writing took second place, and its main purpose, for London, was that of paying for his work on the ranch. The ranch was largely a failure, some say because it was too advanced for the times. The ranch is now a National Historic Landmark and protected as part of the Jack London State Historic Park.

London died at his ranch on 22 November 1916 at the age of 40. His ashes are buried, together with those of his second wife, on his ranch. The grave is marked by a single, simple, mossy boulder.

About the story

The Shadow and the Flash was first published in 1903. It is a tale about two competitive brothers who take different routes to achieving invisibility.

Background information

The science of invisibility

The experiments into the creation of invisibility in the story are based on the following scientific principles.

1 The nature of light

Light travels in waves and is reflected, diffracted and refracted by the objects it meets in its path.

Terms used in the story:

diffraction the process by which sound, water and light waves change when they pass over an object or through a narrow space

refraction when a surface such as water or glass refracts light, light travels in a slightly different direction after it hits the surface, so that the surface appears to bend

light polarisation the process of eliminating vibrations in light waves

sun dogs, wind dogs, rainbows, halos, parhelia examples of optical phenomena which produce multi-coloured, or rainbow, flashes of light when sunlight is refracted by ice, rain or wind.

---

2 The nature of transparency

If an object is transparent, it allows light to pass through it. Air, some gases, liquids such as water, some forms of glass and plastic are transparent.

3 The nature of colour

Visible light is a range of electromagnetic wavelengths that can be seen by the human eye. The range consists of various bands; each band corresponds to a colour range. There are six basic colour bands (from blue at the lowest frequency to red at the highest frequency). The colour of an object depends on the wavelength of the light that is reflected or refracted by it. If all the light that hits the object is reflected, then we see it as white; if all the light is absorbed, we see it as black.

Colourings and pigments are chemical substances that selectively absorb and reflect light at different wavelengths. If only light at the lower end of the range is reflected, we see the object as blue. If only light at the top end of the range is reflected, we see the object as red. If all the light is absorbed we see the object as black.

The colouring depends on the molecular structure of the object and a change in the molecular structure can bring about a change in colour.

Current scientific research into invisibility

Scientists in the UK and USA are working on the creation of an 'invisibility cloak' – a material which could be used to make objects invisible. They are hoping to develop a material which will allow light waves to bend around it without being reflected or absorbed. An early prototype, which is semi-transparent, was first demonstrated in 2006.

Summary

It may help you to know something about what happens in the story before you read it. Don't worry, this summary does *not* tell you how the story ends!

The story tells of three friends, Lloyd, Paul and the story teller. The three boys grew up together and knew each other very well. Lloyd and Paul always competed against each other in everything and the story teller had to try to keep the peace between them.

Once the boys had been swimming in the river with friends. They were playing a game to see who could dive into the river and stay under water the longest. Lloyd and Paul dived in together. They stayed under water so long that the story teller dived in after them. But Lloyd and Paul refused to let go of the roots on the river bed, even though they had both run out of breath. The story teller had to ask the other boys who were with them to help bring them both back up. Lloyd and Paul were very lucky that their friends were there to rescue them. They had nearly drowned because of their rivalry.

At university, Paul and Lloyd both studied Chemistry. They were both excellent students and their constant rivalry pushed them to excel in their studies. They didn't only compete over their studies, they were also rivals in love. They both fell in love with the same woman and their friendship came to an end. However, they both continued to be friends with the story teller.

One day, Lloyd was visiting the story teller at his home, and they started talking about the subject of invisibility, and of a mythical tribe of invisible people. Lloyd believed that the key to creating invisibility was colour. He believed that if he could create a perfect black paint, he could make things, and even people, invisible. Paul overheard the conversation and disagreed with Lloyd. He believed that the key to invisibility was transparency. Lloyd claimed that it was impossible to create transparency. Paul took up the challenge, and both men immediately dedicated themselves to creating invisibility.

Both Lloyd and Paul shared the results of their experiments with the story teller. Lloyd worked hard on creating the perfect black paint. Paul worked hard on creating transparency. First he succeeded with objects and then with animals. The story teller was amazed by the results. At the same time Lloyd finally succeeded in creating a perfect black paint and called the story teller over to see its effects. Again the story teller was amazed by the results.

All this time, the two rivals had kept away from each other, and knew nothing of each other's experiments. However, the time came when they both decided to confront each other, with tragic results.

Pre-reading exercises

Key vocabulary

This section will help you familiarise yourself with some of the more specific vocabulary used in the story. You may want to use it to help you before you start reading, or as a revision exercise after you have finished the story

Rivalry

One of the main themes of the story is the rivalry between the two main characters, Paul and Lloyd.

> **rivalry** a situation in which people, teams, businesses, etc. compete with one another

1 **Look at the words and phrases in bold in the extracts below and match them to their definitions (a) to (j).**

1 *They were always competing, **striving** to **outdo** each other, and when entered upon some such **struggle** there was no limit either to their **endeavors** or passions.*

2 *Neither would let go and **acknowledge** himself **beaten**.*

3 *Their rivalry soon became a noted thing throughout the university. Each was a **spur** to the other, and they went into chemistry deeper than did ever students before.*

4 *My friendship and their **mutual animosity** were the two things that linked them in any way together.*

5 *Both men attacked the problem with all the tremendous energy for which they were noted, and with a **rancor** and bitterness that made me tremble for the success of either.*

(a) to accept or admit that something is real

(b) defeated

(c) an effort to do something new or difficult
(d) to be better than someone else at doing something
(e) a strong feeling of disliking someone
(f) to make a lot of effort to achieve something
(g) an attempt to defeat someone
(h) felt or done in the same way by two or more people
(i) a feeling of anger that lasts a long time
(j) something that encourages someone to do something (literally, a metal object on a horse-rider's shoe that is used to make the horse go faster)

2 Use the words in the box to complete the simplified versions of the sentences above.

admit   anger   better   disliked   efforts   fight   lost   trying   other

1 They were always competing, ... to be .... than each other and each time they got into a .... there was no limit to their .... or their passion.
2 Neither would let go or .... that they had ....
3 The fact that they were both my friends, and that they both .... each .... were the only things they had in common.
4 The two men attacked the problem with incredible energy and equally incredible ....

Verbs of movement

Although the rivalry between the two friends is mainly intellectual, there is also a very physical side to it; this is reflected in the story's use of verbs of movement.

3 Look at the verbs of movement in bold on the next page. Match them with a word or phrase in the box below.

into water   my legs   in the dark   on the step   slowly
down gently   the cat's ears   playfully   my toe   his head against the door
his hand   a tennis ball   from side to side   back to me   violently

brush against to touch something very gently for a very short time as you walk past

butt to hit something with your head

cavort to play, dance or have fun

dart to make a sudden quick movement

fling to throw something very hard

fondle to rub or touch an animal in a gentle way

pitch to fall suddenly in a certain direction

plod to walk with slow heavy steps

plunge 1) to quickly jump or dive, 2) to start doing something with energy and enthusiasm, but sometimes without thinking first

rebound to hit a surface and then move quickly backwards again

stoop to bend the bottom half of your body down

stub to hit the front of your foot against something accidentally in a hard and painful way

stumble to fall or almost fall when you are walking

trip to hit your foot on something and fall

wring to hold and squeeze something very tightly

4 **Use the words above to complete these sentences.**

1 I saw that they were in trouble so I .... into the river and dived down to help.

2 The cat .... gently .... me as I prepared its food.

3 The lights went out and I .... as I looked for a candle.

4 He ran toward the door, ... on the doormat, and fell flat on the floor.

5 I .... across the field with heavy legs.

6 The cat jumped down and walked towards me. I .... it's ears.

7 The two young dogs .... on the beach.

8 I jumped back in pain when I .... my toe against the leg of the chair.

9 He .... his head against the wall in anger and frustration.

10 The boat .... violently in the storm.

11 He fell to his knees and .... his hands in despair.

12 He stood at the gate and .... the stick as far as he could for the dog to run after it.

13 The dog seemed to have gone mad. He was .... backwards and forwards and barking loudly.

14 I threw the ball against the wall and it .... , hitting me in the face.

Idiomatic expressions

The author uses a number of idiomatic expressions in the story. Look at the expressions in **bold** (a) to (h) and match them with their meanings (1) to (8).

a) **a king's ransom:** *French plate glass, made by the great St Gobain Company, and this is the finest piece they ever made. It cost **a king's ransom**.*

b) **as like as two peas:** *They were **as like as two peas**.*

c) **at concert pitch:** *They lived **at concert pitch**.*

d) **be in line for something:** *Well, I have begun my experiments, and I don't mind telling you that I'm right **in line** for it.*

e) **come to a head:** *Things **came to a head** soon enough.*

f) **know something by heart:** *Each knew the whole poem **by heart**.*

g) **run riot:** *My nerves were all awry, and, from the astounding tricks they played me, my senses seemed to have **run riot**.*

h) **my lips are sealed:** *Never, by word or sign, did I convey to either the slightest hint of the other's progress, and they respected me for **the seal** I put upon my **lips**.*

1 so similar as to be almost identical
2 very intensely
3 to memorise something
4 reach a dramatic conclusion
5 to be likely to get or achieve something
6 used to say you will not tell a secret to anyone else
7 to behave in an uncontrolled and strange way
8 a very large amount of money

5 Use the idioms to complete these sentences.

1 .... , I won't tell anyone, I promise.
2 I think he's .... to win the election.
3 When I heard we'd won the lottery, my imagination started to ....
4 He's incredible, he .... the whole of Shakespeare's works .... !
5 The situation suddenly .... when he saw what had happened to his car.

6 It certainly was a very beautiful piece of art, but it had cost them
....

7 Absolutely everything they did, they did .... They never
relaxed, or took it easy.

8 I've never seen twins that are so alike, they're ....

Main themes

Before you read the story, you may want to think about some of the
main themes that come up. The questions will help you think about
the story as you are reading it for the first time. There is more discussion
of the main themes in the *Literary analysis* section after the story.

Rivalry

One of the main themes of the story is competition and rivalry. The
story explores a case of extreme rivalry between friends and its terrible
consequences.

6 As you read the story, think about these questions:

– How did the rivalry between the two boys start?
– In what way did their friends make it worse?
– Could anything have been done to stop them?

The dangers of obsession

Both Paul and Lloyd become completely obsessed by their search for
invisibility. It is the only thing that matters to them. But obsession is
a destructive force and both men pay the full price for their stubborn
behaviour.

7 As you read the story, think about these questions:

– Why did they both become so obsessed with the idea of
invisibility?
– What were the consequences of their obsession? Were they all
bad?

The danger of scientific discoveries

This is a recurring theme in science fiction, since Mary Shelley's *Frankenstein*. Trying to create something that does not already exist in nature (bringing someone back to life as in *Frankenstein*, time travel as in *A Sound of Thunder*, or invisibility as in this story) can be incredibly dangerous. It can be impossible to control a discovery once it has been made, and we can never predict all the consequences.

8 As you read the story, think about these questions:

- What consequences did Paul and Lloyd fail to predict?
- What consequences did the story teller fail to predict?

The Shadow and the Flash

by Jack London

When I look back, I realize what a peculiar friendship it was. First, there was Lloyd Inwood, tall, slender, and finely knit, nervous and dark. And then Paul Tichlorne, tall, slender, and finely knit, nervous and blond. Each was the replica of the other in everything except color[1]. Lloyd's eyes were black; Paul's were blue. Under stress of excitement, the blood coursed[2] olive in the face of Lloyd, crimson in the face of Paul. But outside this matter of coloring[3] they were as like as two peas. Both were high-strung, prone to excessive tension and endurance, and they lived at concert pitch.

But there was a trio involved in this remarkable friendship, and the third was short, and fat, and chunky, and lazy, and, **loath to say**, it was I. Paul and Lloyd seemed born to rivalry with each other, and I to be peacemaker between them. We grew up together, the three of us, and full often[4] have I received the angry blows each intended for the other. They were always competing, striving to outdo each other, and when entered upon[5] some such struggle there was no limit either to their endeavors[6] or passions.

This intense spirit of rivalry obtained[7] in their studies and their games. If Paul memorized one canto[8] of 'Marmion'[9], Lloyd memorized two cantos, Paul came back with three, and Lloyd again with four, till each knew the whole poem by heart. I remember an incident that occurred at the swimming hole – an

1 *US spelling*: British spelling is *colour*
2 *mainly literary*: ran
3 *US spelling*: British spelling is *colouring*
4 *old-fashioned, phrase 'full often'*: very often
5 *old-fashioned*: into
6 *US spelling*: British spelling is *endeavour*
7 *old-fashioned*: existed
8 a section of a long poem
9 an epic poem by Sir Walter Scott

incident tragically significant of the life-struggle between them. The boys had a game of diving to the bottom of a ten-foot pool and holding on by submerged roots to see who could stay under the longest. Paul and Lloyd allowed themselves to be **bantered** into making the descent together. When I saw their faces, set and determined, disappear in the water as they sank swiftly down, I felt a foreboding of something dreadful. The moments sped, the ripples died away, the face of the pool grew placid and untroubled, and neither black nor golden head broke surface in quest[10] of air. We above grew anxious. The longest record of the longest-winded boy had been exceeded, and still there was no sign. Air bubbles trickled slowly upward, showing that the breath had been expelled from their lungs, and after that the bubbles ceased to trickle upward. Each second became interminable, and, unable longer to endure the suspense, I plunged into the water.

I found them down at the bottom, clutching tight to the roots, their heads not a foot apart, their eyes wide open, each glaring fixedly at the other. They were suffering frightful torment, writhing and twisting in the pangs of voluntary suffocation; for neither would let go and acknowledge himself beaten. I tried to break Paul's hold on the root, but he resisted me fiercely. Then I lost my breath and came to the surface, badly scared. I quickly explained the situation, and half a dozen of us went down and by main strength[11] tore them loose. By the time we got them out, both were unconscious, and it was only after much **barrel-rolling** and rubbing and pounding that they finally came to their senses. They would have drowned there, had no one rescued them.

When Paul Tichlorne entered college, he let it be generally understood that he was going in for the social sciences. Lloyd Inwood, entering at the same time, elected to take the same course. But Paul had had it secretly in mind all the time to study the natural sciences, specializing in chemistry, and at the last

10 *mainly literary*: a long difficult search
11 *old-fashioned*: physical force. *Main strength* in modern usage means the most positive quality in a person or thing

moment he switched over. Though Lloyd had already arranged his year's work and attended the first lectures, he at once followed Paul's lead and went in for the natural sciences and especially for chemistry. Their rivalry soon became a noted thing throughout the university. Each was a spur to the other, and they went into chemistry deeper than did ever students before – so deep, in fact, that ere[12] they took their sheepskins[13] they could have stumped any chemistry or 'cow college[14]' professor in the institution, save 'old' Moss, head of the department, and even him they puzzled and edified[15] more than once. Lloyd's discovery of the 'death bacillus' of the sea toad, and his experiments on it with potassium cyanide, sent his name and that of his university ringing round the world; nor was Paul a whit[16] behind when he succeeded in producing laboratory colloids[17] exhibiting amoeba-like activities, and when he cast new light upon the processes of fertilization through his startling experiments with simple sodium chlorides and magnesium solutions on low forms of marine life.

It was in their undergraduate days, however, in the midst of their profoundest plunges into the mysteries of organic chemistry, that Doris Van Benschoten entered into their lives. Lloyd met her first, but within twenty-four hours Paul saw to it that he also made her acquaintance. Of course, they fell in love with her, and she became the only thing in life worth living for. They wooed[18] her with equal ardor[19] and fire, and so intense became their struggle for her that half the student body took to wagering wildly on the result. Even 'old' Moss, one day, after an astounding demonstration in his private laboratory by Paul, was guilty to the extent of a month's salary of backing him to become the bridegroom of Doris Van Benschoten.

12 *old-fashioned*: before
13 *old-fashioned*: graduated. The degree certificates were originally printed on sheepskin
14 *US English*: provincial college or university
15 *formal*: to teach someone something that increases their knowledge
16 *old-fashioned*: not at all
17 *chemistry*: a mixture of substances
18 *old-fashioned*: tried to start a romantic relationship
19 *literary*: very strong feelings of love. British spelling is *ardour*

In the end she solved the problem in her own way, to everybody's satisfaction except Paul's and Lloyd's. Getting them together, she said that she really could not choose between them because she loved them both equally well; and that, unfortunately, since polyandry[20] was not permitted in the United States she would be compelled to forego[21] the honor[22] and happiness of marrying either of them. Each blamed the other for this lamentable outcome, and the bitterness between them grew more bitter.

But things came to a head soon enough. It was at my home, after they had taken their degrees and dropped out of the world's sight, that the beginning of the end came to pass. Both were men of means[23], with little inclination and no necessity for professional life. My friendship and their mutual animosity were the two things that linked them in any way together. While they were very often at my place, they made it a fastidious point to avoid each other on such visits, though it was inevitable, under the circumstances, that they should come upon each other occasionally.

On the day I have in recollection, Paul Tichlorne had been **mooning** all morning in my study over a current scientific review. This left me free to my own affairs, and I was out among my roses when Lloyd Inwood arrived. Clipping and pruning and tacking the climbers on the porch, with my mouth full of nails, and Lloyd following me about and lending a hand now and again, we fell to discussing the mythical race of invisible people, that strange and vagrant[24] people the traditions of which have come down to us. Lloyd warmed to the talk in his nervous, jerky fashion, and was soon interrogating the physical properties and possibilities of invisibility. A perfectly black object, he contended[25], would elude[26] and defy the acutest vision.

20 the custom of having more than one husband
21 *formal*: decide not to do or have something
22 *US spelling*: British spelling is *honour*
23 they had a lot of money and didn't need to work for a living
24 *old-fashioned*: nomadic, travelling around with no fixed home. In modern usage *vagrant* is a noun which means a person who has no home or job
25 *formal*: to claim that something is true
26 *formal*: to manage to escape or hide

"Color is a sensation," he was saying. "It has no objective reality. Without light, we can see neither colors nor objects themselves. All objects are black in the dark, and in the dark it is impossible to see them. If no light strikes upon them, then no light is flung back from them to the eye, and so we have no vision-evidence of their being."

"But we see black objects in daylight," I objected.

"Very true," he went on warmly. "And that is because they are not perfectly black. Were they perfectly black, absolutely black, as it were, we could not see them – ay, not in the blaze of a thousand suns could we see them! And so I say, with the right pigments, properly compounded, an absolutely black paint could be produced which would **render** invisible whatever it was applied to."

"It would be a remarkable discovery," I said non-committally, for the whole thing seemed too fantastic for aught[27] but speculative purposes.

"Remarkable!" Lloyd slapped me on the shoulder. "I should say so. Why, old chap[28], to coat myself with such a paint would be to put the world at my feet. The secrets of kings and courts would be mine, the machinations of diplomats and politicians, the play of stock-gamblers, the plans of trusts and corporations. I could keep my hand on the inner pulse of things and become the greatest power in the world. And I –" He broke off shortly, then added, "Well, I have begun my experiments, and I don't mind telling you that I'm right in line for it."

A laugh from the doorway startled us. Paul Tichlorne was standing there, a smile of **mockery** on his lips.

"You forget, my dear Lloyd," he said.

"Forget what?"

"You forget," Paul went on – "ah, you forget the shadow."

I saw Lloyd's face drop, but he answered **sneeringly**, "I can carry a sunshade, you know."

Then he turned suddenly and fiercely upon him. "Look here, Paul, you'll keep out of this if you know what's good for you."

27 *old-fashioned*: anything
28 *old-fashioned*: an affectionate exclamation used with a male friend

A rupture seemed imminent, but Paul laughed good-naturedly. "I wouldn't lay fingers on your dirty pigments. Succeed beyond your most sanguine[29] expectations, yet you will always fetch up against[30] the shadow. You can't get away from it. Now I shall go on the very opposite **tack**. In the very nature of my proposition the shadow will be eliminated —"

"Transparency!" ejaculated[31] Lloyd, instantly. "But it can't be achieved."

"Oh, no; of course not." And Paul shrugged his shoulders and strolled off down the briar-rose path.

This was the beginning of it. Both men attacked the problem with all the tremendous energy for which they were noted, and with a rancor[32] and bitterness that made me tremble for the success of either. Each trusted me to the utmost, and in the long weeks of experimentation that followed I was made a party to both sides, listening to their theorizings and witnessing their demonstrations. Never, by word or sign, did I convey to either the slightest hint of the other's progress, and they respected me for the seal I put upon my lips.

Lloyd Inwood, after prolonged and **unintermittent** application, when the tension upon his mind and body became too great to bear, had a strange way of obtaining relief. He attended prize fights[33]. It was at one of these brutal exhibitions, whither[34] he had dragged me in order to tell his latest results, that his theory received striking confirmation.

"Do you see that red-whiskered[35] man?" he asked, pointing across the ring to the fifth tier of seats on the opposite side. "And do you see the next man to him, the one in the white hat? Well, there is quite a gap between them, is there not?"

"Certainly," I answered. "They are a seat apart. The gap is the unoccupied seat."

29 *formal*: confident and hopeful about what might happen
30 *informal, phrase 'fetch up against'*: to have to deal with a problem
31 *old-fashioned*: to suddenly say or shout something
32 *US spelling*: British spelling is *rancour*
33 *old-fashioned*: boxing matches
34 *old-fashioned*: where
35 *old-fashioned*: bearded

He leaned over to me and spoke seriously. "Between the red-whiskered man and the white-hatted man sits Ben Wasson. You have heard me speak of him. He is the cleverest pugilist[36] of his weight in the country. He is also a Caribbean negro[37], full-blooded, and the blackest in the United States. He has on a black overcoat buttoned up. I saw him when he came in and took that seat. As soon as he sat down he disappeared. Watch closely; he may smile."

I was for crossing over to verify Lloyd's statement, but he restrained me. "Wait," he said.

I waited and watched, till the red-whiskered man turned his head as though addressing the unoccupied seat; and then, in that empty space, I saw the rolling whites of a pair of eyes and the white double-crescent of two rows of teeth, and for the instant I could make out a negro's face. But with the passing of the smile his visibility passed, and the chair seemed vacant as before.

"Were he perfectly black, you could sit alongside him and not see him," Lloyd said; and I confess the illustration was apt enough to make me well-nigh[38] convinced.

I visited Lloyd's laboratory a number of times after that, and found him always deep in his search after the absolute black. His experiments covered all sorts of pigments, such as lamp-blacks[39], tars, carbonized vegetable matters, soots[40] of oils and fats, and the various carbonized animal substances.

"White light is composed of the seven primary colors," he argued to me. "But it is itself, of itself, invisible. Only by being reflected from objects do it and the objects become visible. But only that portion of it that is reflected becomes visible. For instance, here is a blue tobacco-box. The white light strikes against it, and, with one exception, all its component colors – violet, indigo, green, yellow, orange, and red – are absorbed. The one exception is BLUE. It is not absorbed, but reflected.

36 *old-fashioned*: boxer
37 of black African descent; at the time the story was written it was a normal, neutral term, but it has since come to be considered offensive in most contexts
38 *old-fashioned*: almost
39 the traces of smoke left inside a lamp which has held a bare flame
40 the black powder left over after something has burnt

Wherefore[41] the tobacco-box gives us a sensation of blueness. We do not see the other colors because they are absorbed. We see only the blue. For the same reason grass is GREEN. The green waves of white light are thrown upon[42] our eyes."

"When we paint our houses, we do not apply color to them," he said at another time. "What we do is to apply certain substances that have the property of absorbing from white light all the colors except those that we would have our houses appear. When a substance reflects all the colors to the eye, it seems to us white. When it absorbs all the colors, it is black. But, as I said before, we have as yet no perfect black. All the colors are not absorbed. The perfect black, **guarding against** high lights, will be utterly and absolutely invisible. Look at that, for example."

He pointed to the **palette** lying on his work-table. Different shades of black pigments were brushed on it. One, in particular, I could hardly see. It gave my eyes a **blurring** sensation, and I rubbed them and looked again.

"That," he said impressively, "is the blackest black you or any mortal man ever looked upon. But just you wait, and I'll have a black so black that no mortal man will be able to look upon it – and see it!"

On the other hand, I used to find Paul Tichlorne plunged as deeply into the study of light polarization, diffraction, and interference, single and double refraction, and all manner of strange organic compounds.

"Transparency: a state or quality of body which permits all rays of light to pass through," he defined for me. "That is what I am seeking. Lloyd **blunders** up against the shadow with his perfect opaqueness. But I escape it. A transparent body casts no shadow; neither does it reflect light-waves – that is, the perfectly transparent does not. So, avoiding high lights, not only will such a body cast no shadow, but, since it reflects no light, it will also be invisible."

We were standing by the window at another time. Paul was engaged in polishing a number of lenses, which were **ranged**

41 *old-fashioned*: so, therefore
42 *old-fashioned*: on

along the **sill**. Suddenly, after a pause in the conversation, he said, "Oh! I've dropped a lens. Stick your head out, old man, and see where it went to."

Out I started to thrust my head, but a sharp blow on the forehead caused me to recoil. I rubbed my bruised brow and gazed with reproachful inquiry at Paul, who was laughing in **gleeful**, boyish fashion.

"Well?" he said.

"Well?" I echoed.

"Why don't you investigate?" he demanded. And investigate I did. Before thrusting out my head, my senses, automatically active, had told me there was nothing there, that nothing intervened between me and out-of-doors, that the aperture[43] of the window opening was utterly empty. I stretched forth[44] my hand and felt a hard object, smooth and cool and flat, which my touch, out of its experience, told me to be glass. I looked again, but could see positively nothing.

"White quartzose[45] sand," Paul rattled off, "sodic carbonate[46], slaked lime[47], cutlet[48], manganese peroxide – there you have it, the finest French plate glass, made by the great St Gobain Company[49], who made the finest plate glass in the world, and this is the finest piece they ever made. It cost a king's ransom. But look at it! You can't see it. You don't know it's there till you run your head against it.

"Eh, old boy! That's merely an object-lesson – certain elements, in themselves opaque, yet so compounded as to give a resultant body which is transparent. But that is a matter of inorganic chemistry, you say. Very true. But I dare to assert, standing here on my two feet, that in the organic I can duplicate whatever occurs in the inorganic.

"Here!" He held a test-tube between me and the light, and I noted the cloudy or muddy liquid it contained. He emptied

43 *formal*: a small, narrow hole
44 *old-fashioned*: out
45 made of quartz
46 sodium carbonate
47 calcium hydroxide Ca(OH)2
48 *technical*: broken pieces of glass of mixed colours and types
49 makers of high-quality glass since the 17th century

the contents of another test-tube into it, and almost instantly it became clear and sparkling.

"Or here!" With quick, nervous movements among his array of test-tubes, he turned a white solution to a wine color, and a light yellow solution to a dark brown. He dropped a piece of litmus paper into an acid, when it changed instantly to red, and on floating it in an alkali it turned as quickly to blue.

"The litmus paper is still the litmus paper," he enunciated[50] in the formal manner of the lecturer. "I have not changed it into something else. Then what did I do? I merely changed the arrangement of its molecules. Where, at first, it absorbed all colors from the light but red, its molecular structure was so changed that it absorbed red and all colors except blue. And so it goes, ad infinitum[51]. Now, what I purpose to do is this." He paused for a space. "I purpose to seek – ay, and to find – the proper reagents[52], which, acting upon the living organism, will bring about molecular changes **analogous** to those you have just witnessed. But these reagents, which I shall find, and for that matter, upon which I already have my hands, will not turn the living body to blue or red or black, but they will turn it to transparency. All light will pass through it. It will be invisible. It will cast no shadow."

A few weeks later I went hunting with Paul. He had been promising me for some time that I should have the pleasure of shooting over a wonderful dog – the most wonderful dog, in fact, that ever man shot over, so he averred[53], and continued to aver till my curiosity was aroused. But on the morning in question I was disappointed, for there was no dog in evidence.

"Don't see him about," Paul remarked unconcernedly, and we set off across the fields.

I could not imagine, at the time, what was ailing[54] me, but I had a feeling of some impending and deadly illness. My nerves were all **awry**, and, from the astounding tricks they played me,

50 *formal*: to express an idea clearly and in detail
51 *Latin*: infinitely, for ever
52 *scientific*: a substance used in a chemical reaction
53 *formal*: to say something in a very determined way because you believe strongly in it

my senses seemed to have run riot. Strange sounds disturbed me. At times I heard the swish-swish of grass being shoved aside, and once the **patter** of feet across a patch of stony ground.

"Did you hear anything, Paul?" I asked once.

But he shook his head, and thrust his feet steadily forward.

While climbing a fence, I heard the low, eager **whine** of a dog, apparently from within a couple of feet of me; but on looking about me I saw nothing.

I dropped to the ground, limp and trembling.

"Paul," I said, "we had better return to the house. I am afraid I am going to be sick."

"Nonsense, old man," he answered. "The sunshine has gone to your head like wine. You'll be all right. It's famous[55] weather."

But, passing along a narrow path through a **clump** of **cottonwoods**, some object brushed against my legs and I stumbled and nearly fell. I looked with sudden anxiety at Paul.

"What's the matter?" he asked. "Tripping over your own feet?"

I kept my tongue between my teeth and plodded on, though sore[56] **perplexed** and thoroughly satisfied that some acute and mysterious malady[57] had attacked my nerves. So far my eyes had escaped; but, when we got to the open fields again, even my vision went back on me. Strange flashes of vari-colored[58], rainbow light began to appear and disappear on the path before me. Still, I managed to keep myself in hand, till the vari-colored lights persisted for a space of fully twenty seconds, dancing and flashing in continuous play. Then I sat down, weak and shaky.

"It's all up with me," I gasped, covering my eyes with my hands. "It has attacked my eyes. Paul, take me home."

But Paul laughed long and loud. "What did I tell you? – the most wonderful dog, eh? Well, what do you think?"

He turned partly from me and began to whistle. I heard the patter of feet, the **panting** of a heated animal, and the

54 *old-fashioned*: to make someone ill or unhappy
55 *old-fashioned*: very good
56 *old-fashioned*: extremely
57 *old-fashioned*: an illness
58 multi-coloured

unmistakable **yelp** of a dog. Then Paul stooped down and apparently fondled the empty air.

"Here! Give me your fist."

And he rubbed my hand over the cold nose and **jowls** of a dog. A dog it certainly was, with the shape and the smooth, short coat of a pointer[59].

Suffice to say, I speedily recovered my spirits and control. Paul put a collar about the animal's neck and tied his handkerchief to its tail. And then was vouchsafed[60] us the remarkable sight of an empty collar and a waving handkerchief cavorting over the fields. It was something to see that collar and handkerchief pin[61] a bevy[62] of **quail** in a clump of locusts[63] and remain rigid and immovable till we had flushed[64] the birds.

Now and again the dog emitted the vari-colored light-flashes I have mentioned. The one thing, Paul explained, which he had not anticipated and which he doubted could be overcome.

"They're a large family," he said, "these sun dogs, wind dogs, rainbows, halos, and parhelia[65]. They are produced by refraction of light from mineral and ice crystals, from mist, rain, spray, and no end of things; and I am afraid they are the penalty I must pay for transparency. I escaped Lloyd's shadow only to fetch up against the rainbow flash."

A couple of days later, before the entrance to Paul's laboratory, I encountered a terrible **stench**. So overpowering was it that it was easy to discover the source – a mass of putrescent[66] matter on the doorstep which in general outlines resembled a dog.

Paul was startled when he investigated my find. It was his invisible dog, or rather, what had been his invisible dog, for it was now plainly visible. It had been playing about but a few minutes before in all health and strength. Closer examination

59 a breed of hunting dog
60 *old-fashioned*: offered
61 *a hunting term*: to find and indicate the location of a bird
62 *a hunting term*: a group of birds
63 a type of bush
64 *a hunting term*: made the birds come out of the bush
65 various optical illusions
66 *formal*: decaying and smelling unpleasant

revealed that the skull had been crushed by some heavy blow. While it was strange that the animal should have been killed, the inexplicable thing was that it should so quickly decay.

"The reagents I injected into its system were harmless," Paul explained. "Yet they were powerful, and it appears that when death comes they force practically instantaneous disintegration. Remarkable! Most remarkable! Well, the only thing is not to die. They do not harm so long as one lives. But I do wonder who smashed in that dog's head."

Light, however, was thrown upon this when a frightened housemaid brought the news that Gaffer Bedshaw had that very morning, not more than an hour back, gone violently insane, and was strapped down at home, in the huntsman's **lodge**, where he **raved** of a battle with a ferocious and gigantic beast that he had encountered in the Tichlorne pasture. He claimed that the thing, whatever it was, was invisible, that with his own eyes he had seen that it was invisible; wherefore his tearful wife and daughters shook their heads, and wherefore he but waxed[67] the more violent, and the gardener and the coachman tightened the straps by another hole.

Nor, while Paul Tichlorne was thus successfully mastering the problem of invisibility, was Lloyd Inwood a whit behind. I went over in answer to a message of his to come and see how he was getting on. Now his laboratory occupied an isolated situation in the midst of his vast grounds. It was built in a pleasant little **glade**, surrounded on all sides by a dense forest growth, and was to be gained by way of a winding and erratic path. But I have travelled that path so often as to know every foot of it, and conceive my surprise when I came upon the glade and found no laboratory. The quaint shed structure with its red sandstone chimney was not. Nor did it look as if it ever had been. There were no signs of ruin, no **debris**, nothing.

I started to walk across what had once been its site. "This," I said to myself, "should be where the step went up to the door." Barely were the words out of my mouth when I stubbed my toe on some obstacle, pitched forward, and butted my head into

67 *mainly literary*: to talk a lot in a way that expresses emotion

something that FELT very much like a door. I reached out my hand. It WAS a door. I found the knob and turned it. And at once, as the door swung inward on its hinges, the whole interior of the laboratory impinged upon[68] my vision. Greeting Lloyd, I closed the door and backed up the path a few paces. I could see nothing of the building. Returning and opening the door, at once all the furniture and every detail of the interior were visible. It was indeed startling, the sudden transition from void to light and form and color.

"What do you think of it, eh?" Lloyd asked, wringing my hand. "I slapped a couple of coats of absolute black on the outside yesterday afternoon to see how it worked. How's your head? You bumped it pretty solidly, I imagine."

"Never mind that," he interrupted my congratulations. "I've something better for you to do."

While he talked he began to strip, and when he stood naked before me he thrust a pot and brush into my hand and said, "Here, give me a coat of this."

It was an oily, shellac[69]-like stuff, which spread quickly and easily over the skin and dried immediately.

"Merely preliminary and precautionary," he explained when I had finished; "but now for the real stuff."

I picked up another pot he indicated, and glanced inside, but could see nothing.

"It's empty," I said.

"Stick your finger in it."

I obeyed, and was aware of a sensation of cool moistness. On withdrawing my hand I glanced at the forefinger, the one I had immersed, but it had disappeared. I moved and knew from the alternate tension and relaxation of the muscles that I moved it, but it defied my sense of sight. To all appearances I had been shorn of a finger; nor could I get any visual impression of it till I extended it under the skylight and saw its shadow plainly blotted on the floor.

---

68 *formal*: to have a negative effect on something
69 a type of varnish

Lloyd chuckled. "Now spread it on, and keep your eyes open."

I dipped the brush into the seemingly empty pot, and gave him a long stroke across his chest. With the passage of the brush the living flesh disappeared from beneath. I covered his right leg, and he was a one-legged man defying all laws of gravitation. And so, stroke by stroke, member by member, I painted Lloyd Inwood into nothingness. It was a **creepy** experience, and I was glad when naught[70] remained in sight but his burning black eyes, poised apparently unsupported in mid-air.

"I have a refined and harmless solution for them," he said. "A fine spray with an air-brush, and presto! I am not."

This deftly accomplished, he said, "Now I shall move about, and do you tell me what sensations you experience."

"In the first place, I cannot see you," I said, and I could hear his gleeful laugh from the midst of the emptiness. "Of course," I continued, "you cannot escape your shadow, but that was to be expected. When you pass between my eye and an object, the object disappears, but so unusual and incomprehensible is its disappearance that it seems to me as though my eyes had blurred. When you move rapidly, I experience a bewildering succession of **blurs**. The blurring sensation makes my eyes ache and my brain tired."

"Have you any other warnings of my presence?" he asked.

"No, and yes," I answered. "When you are near me I have feelings similar to those produced by **dank** warehouses, **gloomy crypts**, and deep mines. And as sailors feel the **loom of the land** on dark nights, so I think I feel the loom of your body. But it is all very vague and intangible."

Long we talked that last morning in his laboratory; and when I turned to go, he put his unseen hand in mine with nervous grip, and said, "Now I shall conquer the world!" And I could not dare to tell him of Paul Tichlorne's equal success.

At home I found a note from Paul, asking me to come up immediately, and it was high noon when I came spinning up the

---

70 *old-fashioned:* nothing

driveway on my wheel[71]. Paul called me from the tennis court, and I dismounted and went over. But the court was empty. As I stood there, gaping open-mouthed, a tennis ball struck me on the arm, and as I turned about, another **whizzed** past my ear. For aught I could see of my assailant, they came whirling at me from out of space, and right well was I peppered with them. But when the balls already flung at me began to come back for a second **whack**, I realized the situation. Seizing a racquet and keeping my eyes open, I quickly saw a rainbow flash appearing and disappearing and darting over the ground. I took out[72] after it, and when I laid the racquet upon it for a half-dozen stout blows, Paul's voice rang out:

"Enough! Enough! Oh! Ouch! Stop! You're landing on my naked skin, you know! Ow! O-w-w! I'll be good! I'll be good! I only wanted you to see my **metamorphosis**," he said **ruefully**, and I imagined he was rubbing his hurts.

A few minutes later we were playing tennis – a handicap on my part, for I could have no knowledge of his position save when all the angles between himself, the sun, and me, were in proper conjunction. Then he flashed, and only then. But the flashes were more brilliant than the rainbow – purest blue, most delicate violet, brightest yellow, and all the intermediary shades, with the scintillant[73] brilliancy of the diamond, dazzling, blinding, **iridescent**.

But in the midst of our play I felt a sudden cold chill, reminding me of deep mines and gloomy crypts, such a chill as I had experienced that very morning. The next moment, close to the net, I saw a ball rebound in mid-air and empty space, and at the same instant, a score of feet away, Paul Tichlorne emitted a rainbow flash. It could not be he from whom the ball had rebounded, and with sickening dread I realized that Lloyd Inwood had come upon the scene. To make sure, I looked for his shadow, and there it was, a shapeless **blotch** the **girth** of his body, (the sun was overhead), moving along the ground. I

71 *old-fashioned*: bicycle
72 *old-fashoined*: took off
73 *old-fashioned*: flashing

remembered his threat, and felt sure that all the long years of rivalry were about to culminate in uncanny battle.

I cried a warning to Paul, and heard a **snarl** as of a wild beast, and an answering snarl. I saw the dark blotch move swiftly across the court, and a brilliant burst of vari-colored light moving with equal swiftness to meet it; and then shadow and flash came together and there was the sound of unseen blows. The net went down before my frightened eyes. I sprang toward the fighters, crying:

"For God's sake!"

But their locked bodies smote[74] against my knees, and I was overthrown.

"You keep out of this, old man!" I heard the voice of Lloyd Inwood from out of the emptiness. And then Paul's voice crying, "Yes, we've had enough of peacemaking!"

From the sound of their voices I knew they had separated. I could not locate Paul, and so approached the shadow that represented Lloyd. But from the other side came a stunning blow on the point of my jaw, and I heard Paul scream angrily, "Now will you keep away?"

Then they came together again, the impact of their blows, their groans and gasps, and the swift flashings and shadow-movings telling plainly of the deadliness of the struggle.

I shouted for help, and Gaffer Bedshaw came running into the court. I could see, as he approached, that he was looking at me strangely, but he collided with the combatants and was hurled headlong to the ground. With despairing shriek and a cry of "O Lord, I've got 'em!" he sprang to his feet and tore madly out of the court.

I could do nothing, so I sat up, fascinated and powerless, and watched the struggle. The noonday sun beat down with dazzling brightness on the naked tennis court. And it was naked. All I could see was the blotch of shadow and the rainbow flashes, the dust rising from the invisible feet, the earth tearing up from beneath the straining foot-grips, and the wire screen bulge once or twice as their bodies hurled against it. That was all, and after

74 old-fashioned (smite, smote, smitten): to hit someone or something very hard

a time even that ceased. There were no more flashes, and the shadow had become long and stationary; and I remembered their set boyish faces when they clung to the roots in the deep coolness of the pool.

They found me an hour afterward. Some **inkling** of what had happened got to the servants and they quitted the Tichlorne service in a body. Gaffer Bedshaw never recovered from the second shock he received, and is confined in a madhouse, hopelessly incurable. The secrets of their marvellous discoveries died with Paul and Lloyd, both laboratories being destroyed by grief-stricken relatives. As for myself, I no longer care for chemical research, and science is a **tabooed** topic in my household. I have returned to my roses. Nature's colors are good enough for me.

Post-reading exercises

Understanding the story

1 Use these questions to help you check that you have understood the story.

1 In what ways were Paul and Lloyd similar?
2 In what ways were they different?
3 What was the story teller's role in the three-way friendship?
4 What were the rules of the game the boys played at the swimming hole?
5 Why did the story teller jump into the water?
6 Why wouldn't Paul and Lloyd let go?
7 How did they finally bring the two rivals to the surface?
8 Who first made the decision to study natural sciences?
9 What effect did their rivalry have on their studies?
10 What happened when Lloyd met Doris Van Benschoten?
11 Why could she not choose between them?
12 What effect did this have on the relationship between Lloyd and Paul?
13 What did the two young men do when they finished university?
14 In what way was their lifestyle responsible for what happened next?
15 Why did the story teller and Lloyd start discussing the question of invisibility?
16 Was this the first time Lloyd had thought about the subject?
17 What was Lloyd's theory about colour and invisibility?
18 What did the story teller think of Lloyd's theory?
19 What did Lloyd propose to do if he were invisible?
20 What weakness did Paul point out in Lloyd's theory?
21 What was Paul's proposed solution to the problem of invisibility?
22 Had Paul been interested in exploring the subject of invisibility before overhearing Lloyd's conversation with the story teller?
23 Why did Lloyd take the story teller to a boxing match?
24 How did he convince the story teller of his theory of perfect black?
25 Why, according to Lloyd, would perfect black make objects invisible?
26 Are you convinced by his theory?
27 Was the story teller convinced by his theory?
28 Why did Paul claim that his theory of transparency was better than Lloyd's theory of perfect black?
29 What material proof did Paul give to the story teller?

30 What was Paul trying to prove with the litmus paper?
31 Why did Paul invite the story teller to go hunting?
32 Why did the story teller think he was ill?
33 Why did it take him so long to realise that Paul's dog was invisible?
34 What was the one weakness in Paul's experiment?
35 What happened to the dog after a couple of days?
36 How did it die?
37 What happened to it after its death?
38 Did Paul seem to be upset by the dog's death?
39 How did Lloyd prove his success to the story teller?
40 What happened to the story teller's finger when he dipped it in the second pot of paint?
41 What did the story teller see and feel when he looked at the invisible Lloyd?
42 Why did the story teller say that this was the *last morning in his laboratory*?
43 Why didn't he tell Lloyd about Paul's experiments with his dog?
44 Why did Paul invite the story teller to play tennis?
45 How did the story teller know that Lloyd had joined them?
46 Why didn't the story teller try to stop the fight?
47 Why were the two laboratories destroyed?
48 Do you think the story teller could have done anything to avoid the deaths of his two friends?
49 What is the message of the story?

Language study

The story includes a number of passages where processes and scientific principles are described and explained. The passive is often used to explain these processes, and also to describe some of the strange things that happen to the two main characters.

The passive

Form

We form passive verbs by using *be* + **past participle** (*been*, *done*).

The verb *be* can be in any tense or form.

1 **Look at these examples. Underline the verb** *be* **in each example.**
  Match the examples in bold with the verb forms below.

1 *Paul and Lloyd allowed themselves **to be bantered** into making the descent together.*

2 *The longest record of the longest-winded boy **had been exceeded**, and still there was no sign.*

3 *Since polyandry **was not permitted** in the United States she **would be compelled** to forego the honor and happiness of marrying either of them.*

4 *In the very nature of my proposition the shadow **will be eliminated**.*

5 *White light **is composed** of the seven primary colors.*

6 *Only by **being reflected** from objects do it and the objects become visible.*

7 *While it was strange that the animal **should have been killed**, the inexplicable thing was that it should so quickly decay.*

   a) simple present
   b) simple past
   c) past perfect
   d) present modals
   e) past modals
   f) infinitive
   g) *-ing* form

The passive form places the **object** of an **active verb** as the subject of the same verb in the passive. Look at this example.

   *Paul and Lloyd's friends bantered **them** into making the descent together.*

   ***Paul and Lloyd** were bantered into making the descent together.*

Notice that we do not need to mention their friends. It is obvious from the context who is responsible for the action. However, if we wanted to make it clear who is responsible, or who is the agent of the action, we use *by*.

   *Paul and Lloyd were bantered into making the descent together **by** their friends.*

Use

The passive form is used:
a) When we **don't know** who was responsible for an action, we only know the result of the action.
   *It was strange that the animal **should have been killed** (= we don't know who killed the animal, but we do know it's dead).*
b) When it is **obvious** who is responsible for the action from the context or from shared or common knowledge.
   *Drinking under the age of twenty-one **was not permitted** in the United States (= by the government).*

c) When we want to **emphasise the action** or the result of an action.
You will always fetch up against the shadow. You can't get away from it.
In the very nature of my proposition the shadow **will be eliminated**.
We often use the passive to explain **scientific principles and
processes,** where the emphasis is on **the actions** and **the results of
the actions,** and not on the agents.
'White light **is composed** *of the seven primary colors,' he argued to me.*
'But it is itself, of itself, invisible. Only by **being reflected** *from objects
do it and the objects become visible. But only that portion of it that* **is
reflected** *becomes visible.'*

2 **Complete the extracts using a passive form of the verbs in
brackets.**

1 *Air bubbles trickled slowly upward, showing that the breath* ....
(expel) from their lungs.
2 *An absolutely black paint* .... *(could/produce) which would
render invisible whatever it* .... *(apply) to.*
3 *Both men attacked the problem with all the tremendous energy for which
they* .... *(note).*
4 *We do not see the other colors because they* .... *(absorb). We see
only the blue. For the same reason grass is GREEN. The green waves of
white light* .... *(throw) upon our eyes.*
5 *He pointed to the palette lying on his work-table. Different shades of black
pigments* .... *(brush) on it.*
6 *At times I heard the swish-swish of grass* .... *(shove) aside, and
once the patter of feet across a patch of stony ground.*

3 **Complete the (b) sentences so that they mean the same as the (a)
extracts.**

1 *'Transparency!' ejaculated Lloyd, instantly.*
   a) *'But it can't be achieved.'*
   b) *'You* ....*"*
   Which version, (a) or (b), gives more emphasis to the absolute
   impossibility of achieving transparency? Why?
2 *When a substance reflects all the colors to the eye, it seems to us white.
When it absorbs all the colors, it is black. But, as I said before, we have
as yet no perfect black.*
   a) *All the colors are not absorbed.*
   b) *The black we have* ....
   Which version, (a) or (b), emphasises:
   1 the action of absorbing all the colours?
   2 the colour black?

3 a) *The longest record of the longest-winded boy had been exceeded, and still there was no sign.*
   b) They had ....

   Which version, (a) or (b), emphasises how much time had passed?

Inversion after *so*

The intensifying adverb *so* is used to emphasise the extreme quality of an adjective.

So black *that no mortal man will be able to look on it – and see it!*

Form

When the adjective is placed as the beginning of a sentence or clause, the subject and verb are inverted. Compare these two sentences.

Their struggle became so intense …

So intense became their struggle …

Use

Bringing the adjective phrase to the beginning of the sentence emphasises it even more and can create a particularly dramatic effect. Its use is particularly common in literary styles.

4 Rewrite the sentences, starting with the *so* phrase in bold.

1 They had studied **so hard** that they knew more than any of the professors at their college.
2 It will be **so black** that no man will be able to look on it and see it!
3 The smell was **so overpowering** that it was easy to discover the source.
4 Its disappearance is **so unusual** that it seems to me as though my eyes had blurred.
5 Their rivalry was **so strong** it ended up killing them both.
6 Their story was **so incredible** that no one would believe it.

Multiple-clause sentences

The use of multiple-clause sentences is a characteristic feature of London's style in *The Shadow and the Flash*. Background events and stories are often summarised in sentences of five clauses or more.

Look at this example:

> *If Paul memorized one canto of 'Marmion', Lloyd memorized two cantos, Paul came back with three, and Lloyd again with four, till each knew the whole poem by heart.*

The sentence has five clauses and can be broken down into five simple sentences.

1 Paul memorised one canto of 'Marmion'.
2 Lloyd memorised two cantos.
3 Paul came back with three.
4 Lloyd came back again with four.
5 Eventually they both knew the whole poem by heart.

5 Look at a second example. The clauses have been marked for you. Rewrite them as five separate sentences.

I found them down at the bottom, / clutching tight to the roots, / their heads not a foot apart, / their eyes wide open, / each glaring fixedly at the other.

One of the longest and most complicated sentences in the story tells of Gaffer Bedshaw's encounter with the invisible dog. The sentence has been divided into ten sections. Put the sections back in the right order. The first has been done for you.

1 *Light, however, was thrown upon this*
  not more than an hour back,
  when a frightened housemaid brought the news
  that he had encountered in the Tichlorne pasture.
  with a ferocious and gigantic beast
  in the huntsman's lodge,
  that Gaffer Bedshaw had that very morning,
  gone violently insane,
  where he raved of a battle
  and was strapped down at home,

Literary analysis

Plot

1 What are the main events in the story? Write a one-sentence summary of the story.

2 Look at the list of events below. What happened each time? Why are these events important?
   - swimming with friends
   - meeting Doris Van Benschoten
   - a conversation at the story teller's house
   - the boxing match
   - going hunting
   - the game of tennis

3 What happens at the end of the story? Do you think this could have been avoided? Do you agree that the story teller was partly responsible for their deaths?

4 What is the story's message?

Character

5 What do you know about the three main characters? How old are they? What is their social class? What do they do for a living? How do these things contribute to the tragedy?

6 In what ways are Paul and Lloyd similar? In what ways are they different?

7 Why is Lloyd interested in finding a solution to the problem of invisibility? What is he planning to do with this discovery? What is Paul's motivation? Do you sympathise with either of them?

8 Think about the story teller. In what ways is he different from his two friends? In what ways is he similar? What is his role in the three-way friendship?

Narration

9 The story is told in the first person, by a close friend of the two main characters. In what way would it have been told differently if it had been told:
   a) in the diary of one or both of the main characters?
   b) by one of Paul or Lloyd's relatives?
   c) by a person who was not personally involved, for example a local reporter?

Think about what facts would or would not be included, what opinions might be given, what conclusions could be drawn.

10   As the story progresses, the story teller uses more and more dialogue. Find examples of how the dialogue is used to:
a) explain the scientific basis of the experiments
b) show the characters' attitudes to the experiments.
What else do we learn about the characters through their words?

11   What is the narrator's attitude to the competition between Paul and Lloyd? Is he interested in the scientific side of their experiments? Do you think he would like to become invisible too?

Style

12   The author uses a lot of repetition, both within sentences and echoed through the story. Look at the opening paragraph where the story teller introduces the two main characters. What effect does the repetition have? What characteristic is he emphasising? Why is this important in the story?

When I look back, I realize what a peculiar friendship it was. First, there was Lloyd Inwood, tall, slender, and finely knit, nervous and dark. And then Paul Tichlorne, tall, slender, and finely knit, nervous and blond. Each was the replica of the other in everything except color. Lloyd's eyes were black; Paul's were blue. Under stress of excitement, the blood coursed olive in the face of Lloyd, crimson in the face of Paul.

13   Look at the next paragraph, where the story teller introduces and describes himself. Notice how his description mirrors the sentence structure used in the description of Paul and Lloyd. What effect does this have?

14   Look at the description of the incident in the river [page 164]. Notice the details the story teller describes, and the sequence of actions as they wait for the two boys to appear. What kind of reaction is the author trying to create in the reader? Is it effective?

15   Think of how this early scene is a miniature version of the story itself. Look at how it is echoed later in the story:

There were no more flashes, and the shadow had become long and stationary; and I remembered their set boyish faces when they clung to the roots in the deep coolness of the pool.

How does this scene help us understand the story, and, in particular, the ending?

16   Look at the dialogue between the story teller, Paul and Lloyd, where the idea of invisibility is first discussed [pages 166–167]. Notice how the author makes use of questions and objections to break up the scientific details. What is the function of the questions, the objections and the interruptions? What do they tell us about the three men? In what way does the dialogue warn us of what is going to happen next?

17   Look at the passages where the story teller describes the first successful experiments. Find examples of how he uses the sense of touch, smell and hearing to describe his impressions of the invisible dog, the invisible laboratory and the sensations he describes to the newly-painted Paul. What does he see and what does he not see? How effective is his description? How realistic do you think it is? Which details do you find most convincing?

18   Look at the closing passage. What echoes are there from earlier in the story? Notice how the shadow and the flash of the title are used in the description. What sense or senses does the story teller use most to describe the final battle between the two rivals? What effect does this have?

Guidance to the above literary terms, answer keys to all the exercises and activities, plus a wealth of other reading-practice material, can be found on the student's section of the Macmillan Readers website at: www.macmillanenglish.com/readers.

Essay questions

Language analysis

Discuss two or more of the language areas you have studied and explain how they contribute to the narrative style of one or more of the stories in the collection.

Analysing the question

What is the question asking?

It is asking you to:
- choose two or more language areas from the index
- explain both the grammar and the function of the language areas
- use examples from one or more of the stories in the collection.

Preparing your answer

1 Look back through the *Language analysis* sections of the stories you have read and choose several language areas that you feel confident about.
2 Make notes about the language areas. Include notes on form, function and use.
3 Choose examples of the form in one or more stories.
4 Look back at the question and your notes and plan your essay. Use the structure of the question to structure your essay. Here is an example:

Introduction	Introduce the areas you are going to describe.
Main body 1	Explain the general structure and function of the areas you have chosen, use examples.
Main body 2	Analyse how the forms contribute to the narrative style of the story or stories, referring to specific passages in the stories.
Conclusion	Summarise the literary use and function of the language areas you focused on.

Literary analysis

> Choose two or more of the stories in the collection. Look at the new technology or scientific discovery described in the stories and explain how the authors makes each of them seem real. Think about the use of characters, situations and/or imagery.

Analysing the question

What is the question asking?

It is asking you to:
- look at two or more stories in the collection
- discuss the technological or scientific developments which are described in the story
- comment on how the author describes the developments and their consequences.

Preparing your answer

1 Choose one or more stories. Make notes about the science behind the stories and how they relate to the plot, the characters and the main themes.
2 Find key scenes in the stories where the discovery is discussed or illustrated. Make notes about the situations the author describes and any images used. Make a note of any useful quotations.
3 Make notes about your reaction to the stories and their themes.
4 Read the question again and write a plan for your essay. Here is an example:

Introduction	Briefly introduce the stories and the scientific discoveries they explore.
Part 1	Discuss the plot and the situations and how realistic they seem to you.
Part 2	Discuss the characters and/or imagery and how they help bring the story alive.
Conclusion	Make a general comment about the importance of realism in science fiction.

For tips on writing academic essays, and essays about literary analysis, visit the student's section of the Macmillan Readers' website at www.macmillanenglish.com/readers.

Glossary

The definitions in the glossary refer to the meanings of the words and phrases as they are used in the short stories in this collection. Some words and phrases may also have other meanings which are not given here. The definitions are arranged in the story they appear, and in alphabetical order.

We Can Remember It For You Wholesale

artifact (n) an object that was made a long time ago and is historically important

attire (n) *formal*: the clothes that someone is wearing

aversion (n) *formal*: a strong feeling that you don't like someone

burly (adj) a burly man is fat and strong

craving (n) a very strong feeling of wanting something

crossness (n) irritiability or anger

crouch down (v) to move your body close to the ground by bending your knees and leaning forwards slightly

dial (v) to press the numbers on a phone in order to call someone

doomed (adj) certain to fail

drawl (v) to speak slowly with long vowels

drowsily (adv) sleepily

ellipse (n) a shape similar to a circle but longer than it is wide

embossed (adj) decorated with a raised design

feigned (adj) pretending to have a particular feeling

flush (v) if someone flushes, their face turns red because they are hot or ill, or feeling angry, excited or embarrassed

franked (adj) with a stamp or mark that shows that the charge for posting has been paid

glibly (adv) without careful thought

impede (v) stop

inasmuch as PHRASE used for adding a comment that explains or makes clearer what you have just said

jab (v) to push something with a sudden, straight movement, usually with your finger

lamely (adv) in a way that does not seem sincere

lingering (adj) lasting for a long time

memento (n) something that you keep to remind you of a particular person, place or experience

moribund (adj) dying

morose (adj) feeling unhappy, not wanting to talk to anyone

mumble (n) to say something in a way that is not loud or clear so that your words are difficult to understand

mundane (adj) ordinary and not interesting or exciting

ominous (adj) making you think that something bad will happen

pious (adj) very good or moral

polychromatic (adj) multi-coloured

ponder (v) think about a problem or question

quaint (adj) interesting or attractive with a slightly strange and old-fashioned quality

scorn (n) a feeling that someone or something is not good enough to deserve your approval or respect

scornfully (adv) with no respect

scrutinize (v) to examine something very carefully

shimmer (v) to reflect a gentle light that seems to shake slightly

snigger (v) to laugh quietly

sprint (v) run very fast

spurious (adj) not based on true facts

squabble (v) to argue with someone about something that is not important

stalk (v) to walk in a way that shows you are offended or angry

tinker (v) to interfere with something or make small changes to it

trudge (v) to walk with slow, heavy footsteps

wipe out (v) to destroy or kill

writhe (v) to move by twisting and turning, especially when you feel a lot of pain

yearning (n) a strong feeling of wanting something you can't have

A Sound of Thunder

aflame (adj) on fire

annihilate (v) to destroy a group of people or things completely

aurora (n) a phenomenon which produces light which flashes and is full of colours, such as the Aurora Borealis or Aurora Australis at the North and South Poles respectively

bonfire (n) a large fire built outside for burning waste

cavernous (adj) very large and dark

crush (v) to flatten something completely

curse (v) to use offensive or impolite language, especially when angry

drench (v) to make something very wet

envelop (v) to surround someone or something completely

flicker (v) if a light flickers, it does not burn evenly, or it goes on and off

grunt (v) to make a short low sound in your throat and nose at the same time

gauze (n) white cotton cloth that is very thin and is used for protecting and treating an injury

gush (n) a large quantity of liquid that quickly flows out of a place

howl (n) the long loud sound that a dog or similar animal makes

quaver (v) to shake or move slightly (also used to describe your voice when you are feeling afraid or nervous)

lash (v) to hit something with a strong force

link (n) a connection between two or more people, places, facts or events

lunge (v) to move suddenly and with a lot of force, in order to hit or catch something or someone

mate (v) used in biology to describe when animals look for a reproductive partner

moan (v) to make a low sound as if in pain

moss (n) a soft green or brown plant that grows in layers in the wet ground, rocks or trees

nudge (v) to give something a little push with a part of your body, for example your foot or your elbow

plead (v) to ask for something in an emotional way

poised (adj) graceful, controlled yet relaxed

remit (v) give money back

resilient (adj) very strong

settle (v) to stop moving

slay (v) literary, to kill someone in a violent way

snap (v) 1 to break something with a short, loud noise; 2 to speak in a sudden, angry way

snort (v) to make a sudden loud noise through your nose, for example because you are angry or laughing

spurt (v) if a liquid spurts from something it comes out in a sudden strong flow

stagnating (adj) something that is not fresh and is beginning to smell bad

stench (n) strong, unpleasant smell

stomp (v) to stand heavily on something

swamp (n) an area of land covered by water where trees and plants grow

taint (n) something that has been spoilt or that has gone wrong

tangle (n) the untidy shape that things make when they are twisted round each other or round something else

tar (n) a thick, black liquid made from coal, used especially for making the surfaces of roads

tar pit (n) a hole full of tar

teeming (adj) containing or consisting of an extremely large number of people, animals or objects that are all moving around

thrill (n) a feeling of being very excited

wild boar (n) a wild pig

Travel By Wire!

consternation (n) a shocked or worried feeling often caused when something unexpected happens

curdle (v) if milk or another liquid curdles, or is made to curdle, lumps appear in it

dependent (n) child or other family member you give food, money and a home to (British spelling: dependant)

deplorable (adj) extremely bad and shocking

dissipate (v) to gradually disappear

endure (v) suffer

freight (n) goods (objects produced for sale) that are carried by vehicles

gruesome (adj) involving or describing death or injury in a very unpleasant way

inoculated (adj) injected with a small amount of a disease in order to create immunity

insubordination (n) disobedience, not following orders or instructions

lure (v) to persuade someone to do something by making it seem very attractive

mishap (n) a minor mistake or accident

post-mortem (n) autopsy, an examination of a dead body to find the cause of death

rear (v) to look after a child or young animal until it has grown to be an adult

rider (n) an addition to a statement or official document

row (n) noise, noisy behaviour or activity

stuffed (adj) a dead animal that is stuffed has been filled with a substance to make it look alive

synchronize (v) to make two or more things happen or move at the same time

vile (adj) extremely unpleasant

The Martian Odyssey

alight (v) to land

ant-heap (n) where ants live

arc light (n) *old-fashioned:* a light that is produced when electricity flows between two separated points

bingo! (exclamation) used for expressing surprise or excitement at successfully doing something

blamed (adj) *informal, old-fashioned:* an alternative form of 'damned', used for emphasising that you are annoyed

blobby (adj) irregular in shape

blooey! (exclamation) used to mean that something is broken or finished

buzz along (v) to move quickly and easily at a steady pace

ditch (n) a long narrow hole at the side of a road or field, usually for water to run into

cask (n) a round wooden container for storing liquid, especially alcoholic drink

catch the drift PHRASE to understand what someone is saying

clinch (v) to make you decide to do something you were already thinking about

clincher (n) something that settles an argument, makes you take a particular decision, or helps you achieve something

corruption (n) *literary:* the process of decay, especially in a dead body

cramped (adj) small and crowded

cranky (adj) likely to stop working at any time

crevice (n) a narrow crack in a rock or in a wall

desolate (adj) a desolate place is completely empty with no people or pleasant features in it

diaphragm (n) a thin membrane which closes or separates a section in a tube or other cylindrical object

fiendish (adj) very clever but very cruel

flurry (n) a short period of action or emotion

freak (n) something with very unusual features that make it very different from other things of its type

frostbitten (adj) affected by frostbite, a medical condition in which cold weather seriously damages your fingers, toes, ears or nose

fuzz (n) a lot of short soft hairs or fibres like hair

gape (v) to look at something or someone with your mouth open because you are very surprised

get the hang of PHRASE to learn a skill or activity

ground (v) past participle of the verb to grind, to break something into very small pieces or powder, by using a machine or by crushing it between two hard surfaces

haul (v) to pull or carry something heavy with a lot of effort

heave (v) to push, pull or lift a heavy object using a lot of effort

insidious (adj) dangerous because it seems to be harmless or unimportant but in reality causes harm or damage

iron rations (n) a supply of emergency food, especially as used by the armed forces

jitters (n) a nervous, upset feeling caused by not knowing what will happen

labyrinth (n) a place where there are a lot of paths or passages and you can easily get lost

longing (n) a strong feeling of wanting someone or something

mangled (adj) seriously damaged by being twisted or crushed so that it loses its original shape

member (n) part of the body

mimicry (n) the action of pretending to be someone or something else

nondescript (adj) very ordinary and not interesting or attractive

outcropping (n) a rock, or group of rocks, that sticks up out of the ground

pal (n) *informal, old-fashioned*: a friend

pedestal (n) a base on which something such as a statue stands

peep (n) a quick look at something

plain (n) a large, flat area of land

plateau (n) a large, flat area of land that is higher than the land around it

plow along (v) to continue doing something that takes a lot of effort (British spelling: plough)

plug along (v) to continue doing something in a determined way

pouch (n) a small bag made of cloth or thin leather

pound (v) to hit something several times with a lot of force

prey (n) an animal that is caught by another animal and eaten

quit (v) to stop working

rap (v) to hit something hard and quickly

rig up (v) to make something quickly out of whatever you can find

rigmarole (n) a description or story that is longer and more complicated than it needs to be

scout about (v) to search or examine a place, area or situation to get information about it

sift (v) to pour a dry substance through a sieve (a net of very thin wires on a ring) to remove the large pieces

shipshape (adj) tidy and in good condition

shudder (v) your body suddenly shakes, for example because you suddenly feel cold or frightened

smattering (n) a small amount of something

sneak (v) to move somewhere quietly and secretly so that no one can see you or hear you

spore (n) a structure consisting of one cell that is produced by a plant such as a mushroom and can develop into a new living thing of the same type

sputter (v) to speak or say something in a confused way, often while taking short quick breaths, for example because you are shocked or angry

spurt (n) a sudden strong flow of a liquid

squirt (v) to make a liquid move with a lot of force

stir up (v) to make water or dust move around

stroll (n) a slow walk for pleasure

stuffy (adj) too warm and without enough fresh air

tame (adj) a tame animal has been trained to stay calm when people are near it, because it is used to being with them

tangled (adj) twisted around each other in an untidy way

tenuous (adj) weak

tumbleweed (n) a round plant that grows in dry areas and rolls when it is blown by the wind

wart (n) a small, hard lump that grows on your skin, for example on your neck or hand, and is caused by a virus

wither (v) to become weaker or smaller and then disappear

writhe (v) to move by twisting and turning, especially when you are in a lot of pain

zenith (n) the point in the sky where the sun or moon is highest above the Earth

The Shadow and the Flash

analogous (adj) similar to another situation, process, etc so that the same things are true of both

awry (adj) not in the correct position, not functioning correctly

banter (v) friendly conversation in which people tell jokes to each other

bantered (adj) persuaded into doing something by means of banter

barrel-rolling (n) rolling someone backwards and forwards like a barrel

blotch (n) a coloured mark on something

blunder (v) to make a careless or embarrassing mistake

blur (n) a shape that is difficult to see clearly, for example because it is moving too fast

blur (v) if a thing blurs, or if something blurs it, it becomes difficult to see it clearly, often because its edges are not clear

clump (n) a group of trees or plants growing close together

cottonwood (n) a North American tree that has seeds covered in fibres that look like cotton wool (soft cotton, usually white, used for cleaning a cut in your skin or removing make-up)

creepy (adj) unpleasant in a way that makes you feel nervous or frightened

crypt (n) an underground room where the bodies of dead people are buried, usually under a church

dank (adj) a dank room is unpleasant because it is dark and has wet walls

debris (n) the broken pieces that are left when something large has been destroyed

girth (n) the width of a body

glade (n) an area of a forest where there are no trees or bushes

gleeful (adj) happy and excited, often because of someone else's bad luck

gloomy (adj) dark in a way that makes you feel sad or a little afraid

guard against (v) avoid

inkling (n) a slight idea or small piece of information that tells you that something might exist or be happening

iridescent (adj) showing changing colours in different types of light

jowls (n) the loose skin on an animal's cheeks and around its mouth

loath to say PHRASE unwilling to admit to something

lodge (n) a small house built on the land belonging to a large house, often a home to the gardener, or other servants involved in looking after the grounds of the house

loom of the land PHRASE a vague and often exaggerated first appearance of something seen in darkness or fog, especially at sea

metamorphosis (n) a major change that makes someone or something very different

mockery (n) remarks or behaviour intended to make someone feel stupid

moon (v) to spend time doing nothing useful or important

palette (n) a board an artist uses for mixing paints

panting (n) the sound of a dog breathing after it has been running

patter (n) the sound of an animal or small child walking or running

perplexed (adj) confused

ranged (adj) displayed in a row

rave (v) to talk in an angry and uncontrolled way

render (v) to make someone or something be or become something

ruefully (adv) in a way that shows you are sorry about something and wish it hadn't happened

quail (n) a small bird that people shoot and eat

sill (n) window sill, a narrow shelf at the bottom of a window

snarl (n) an angry sound, similar to that made by a dog

sneeringly (adv) in an unpleasant way showing no respect

stench (n) a very strong and unpleasant smell

tabooed (adj) if something is tabooed, people do not do it or talk about it because it is offensive or shocking

tack (n) direction

unintermittent (adj) happening regularly, often, or without end

whack (n) the act of hitting something with great force

whine (n) a sound a dog makes to express its feelings

whizz (v) to move or travel very quickly

yelp (n) a short loud noise made by a dog, for example because it is excited, angry or in pain

Dictionary extracts adapted from the Macmillan English Dictionary © Macmillan Publishers Limited 2002

Language study index